LIVING THE LIFE MORE FABULOUS

Beauty, Style & Empowerment for Older Women

A HANDBOOK

TRICIA CUSDEN

For my special granddaughter India, whose birth inspired me to start a fabulous new chapter of my life.

First published in Great Britain in 2018
by Orion Spring an imprint of The Orion
Publishing Group Ltd, Carmelite House,
50 Victoria Embankment, London EC4Y 0DZ

An Hachette UK Company

10 9 8 7 6 5 4 3 2 1

Text copyright © Tricia Cusden 2018
Design and layout nic&lou © Orion
Publishing Group Ltd 2018

Photographs by: Ronnie Temple: 19, 28/29,
39, 41, 45, 46. 92, 93, 111, 119, 120, 121,
122, 222, 234; Simon Songhurst: 3, 5,
11, 15, 22, 35, 39, 43, 49, 55, 65, 83,
89, 109, 117, 134, 136, 141, 147, 159, 165,
175, 178, 188, 189. 210, 213, 217; Beatrix
Blaise: 69; Heidi Alexander: 128/129;
Nicky Emmerson: 67; Getty Images: 16,
38, 40, 62, 74, 79, 96, 99, 103, 107, 141,
154; Shutterstock: 12/13, 21/22, 24/25,
37, 50, 113, 127, 128/129, 132, 172, 184,
192/193, 199, 200/201, 202, 203, 204,
222/223, 234/235; Supplied by Tricia:
25, 53, 66, 67, 136, 147, 151, 173; Hennika
Photography: 201; And thanks also to Mary
(page 20/21), Corinne (page 162) Janet
(pages 192/193) and Lindsay (173) for the
use of their photos.

Printed in China

The moral right of Tricia Cusden to be
identified as the author of this work has been
asserted in accordance with the Copyright,
Designs and Patents Act of 1988.

Every effort has been made to ensure that
the information in the book is accurate.
The information in this book may not be
applicable in each individual case so it is
advised that professional medical advice
is obtained for specific health matters and
before changing any medication or dosage.
Neither the publisher nor author accepts any
legal responsibility for any personal injury or
other damage or loss arising from the use of
the information in this book. In addition if you
are concerned about your diet or exercise
regime and wish to change them, you should
consult a health practitioner first.

A CIP catalogue record for this book is
available from the British Library.

ISBN: 978 1 4091 72697

www.orionbooks.co.uk

Contents

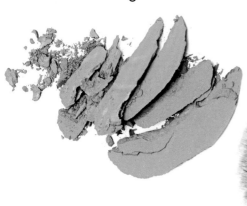

Introduction

There has never been a better time to be an older woman. We are fitter, healthier and living longer than at any time in history. Many of us can now expect to enjoy this further lease of life, so this handbook is designed to show you how to live your extra bonus of time as fabulously as possible. I have chosen to call this a handbook rather than a rule book, because at our age we have surely earned the right not to be told what we should and shouldn't do. Above all, I want this book to inspire you to celebrate rather than bemoan your ageing face, body and self.

Our society seems to value older women only if they are ageing youthfully. Older women must have 'ageless style', whatever that means, and keep fighting the seven, eight, nine or however many signs of ageing you are not supposed to have. You won't find that narrative in this book because I want fifty to be the new fifty (or sixty or seventy) but *as it is now*, not as it was for our parents' generation. I also want this book to reassure you that it is possible to age well so that you can be less fearful about getting older. And, finally, I want it to provide you with lots of hints, tips and suggestions, especially if you are looking for ideas to update your look, improve your general wellbeing or take an exciting or much-needed new direction in your life. In short, I want it to be about two things that have always been very dear to my heart: transformation and empowerment.

My Own Transformation

Before we start, let me tell you briefly about my own transformation since turning sixty-five in December 2012.

As is true for many people, my total change of direction was inspired by a bruising year. In January 2012, my fourth grandchild India was born. Although apparently fine at birth, she was discovered to have a rare chromosomal abnormality and needed intensive care in hospital for several months. Many times, her life hung by a thread. I was needed most days for some form of support, either to India's mother, my daughter Suzy, or to India's two-year-old sister Freya, or to be at India's bedside in hospital. I have never been more aware of the tenuous hold we all have on life, or the importance of not wasting a single moment of the life that we are privileged to have.

When the crisis of India's survival passed and she began to improve and even to thrive, I knew that I couldn't resume the life that I'd had before she was born. I had given up all my work commitments and without the daily need to care for my family, I was at a complete loss as to how to fill my time. I flirted with a few ideas. Maybe I could train to

> **I have always loved makeup and enjoyed the world of business and I greatly dislike the ageism of the beauty industry.**

become a magistrate – but it turned out that I was too old (!). Maybe I could learn to play bridge – but I didn't have anyone to partner with. I kept thinking: 'I might live for another thirty years – how can I create a life which has meaning and purpose?' The main requirement was that my new venture would get me off my sofa, out of my house and well outside my comfort zone. I have always been entrepreneurial and liked risk-taking, so I decided to combine two loves and one hate. I have always loved makeup and enjoyed the world of business and I greatly dislike the ageism of the beauty industry.

I was initially motivated by the frustration of sourcing makeup that worked well on my sixty-five-year-old face. After reading a recommendation in a magazine, I bought a foundation that would apparently make my skin look 'fresh and luminous'. The same day I bought a cream blusher for a total cost of around £50. Both were from high-end brands and, as a lifelong makeup junkie, I knew how to apply both products, but oh what a cruel disappointment when I looked in the mirror! The foundation was too thin to unify my skin tone or cover my acne rosacea, and the blusher just disappeared without trace after a few minutes. I threw both of them into a drawer with disgust and bitterness at the waste of money.

At the same time I had also become deeply offended by the way that the beauty industry only seemed to be interested in selling me something with an 'anti-ageing' label attached. I hated the casually ageist assumption that I must want to do everything in my power to turn back the clock. I was quite happy being in my mid-sixties and had no desire to look younger, so I resented the implication that I must want to 'fight' ageing by using some miracle cream (as if!).

At a Mother's Day lunch in March 2013, I floated the idea of creating a makeup range for older women to my daughters, Anna and Suzy.

I said, 'Tell me if you think I'm mad and I won't do it!' Their immediate reaction was, 'Mum – that's a brilliant idea – go for it!' The next day I came up with the brand name Look Fabulous Forever and registered the domain so that I could create a website. Now I just needed some cosmetics that would actually work with, rather than fight, the changes that happen as we age.

After finding a UK-based cosmetics manufacturer and testing, refining and developing a small range of excellent products, Look Fabulous Forever was born. I decided to make two tutorial videos in order to explain the products and show how brilliantly they worked on a real older face, preferably one which hadn't had lots of 'work' done. So I invited two of my oldest friends (by which I mean I'd known them for years) to come along to a studio so that we could film the transformational effect of the makeup. When the videos were edited, the video maker suggested posting them on YouTube. My initial reaction was entirely negative and quite dismissive. I am not a well-known makeup artist, Look Fabulous Forever was a new and unknown brand and I was featuring my friends – not celebrities. So who would possibly watch them? Fortunately, I couldn't have been more wrong! Within about four months my two makeup videos were being watched by thousands of women every day and were being widely shared. Look Fabulous Forever was on the map and suddenly our online business took off. Since then it has gone from strength to strength and our videos have been seen by millions. As we reach more and more like-minded women, so the word gets spread all over the world.

From the very beginning I have written a weekly blog on things that interest me as a woman of a certain age growing old in an ageist but rapidly changing society. Above all, I wanted my blogs to be a conversation with other like-minded, and sometimes not-so-like-minded, women. My blogs are rarely planned; I prefer inspiration to strike from one week to the next. That way I can respond to what is going on in my own life and also in the world. Yes, I do write about makeup and style, but I also write about health and wellbeing and attitude, and occasionally I will go completely off-piste and write about things like my love of fast cars. In fact, a blog post which I called 'Speed Freak Granny' is my most popular to date, receiving hundreds of comments – every single one urging me to buy the sporty motor I was dithering over for fear of looking ridiculous 'at my age'. Reader, I bought the car.

Even at the planning stage I knew that I wanted Look Fabulous Forever to be about more than makeup. It may sound grandiose but I really wanted the business to give me a voice so that I could inspire older women to feel validated and relevant, rather than marginalised and a bit lost. I also wanted it to give me a platform from which I could challenge some of the lazy and casual assumptions of our ageist society. I wanted to offer a different version of ageing, just as I was offering older women a different version of makeup from that sold by the traditional beauty companies. I wanted to say: 'You are still fabulous despite the odd age spot or wrinkle, so don't let the anti-ageing rhetoric of the beauty industry make you feel bad about yourself.' I had absolutely no idea whether

Within about four months my two makeup videos were being watched by thousands of women every day and were being widely shared.

this would strike a chord with any other women of my generation, but I decided to back my hunch that my messages about embracing rather than fighting our ageing selves would resonate with enough people to make Look Fabulous Forever a viable proposition. I am delighted to say that all of that has transpired.

This book arose from the engagement and interest I receive daily from older women worldwide, and it is my sincere wish that it will excite, inform, inspire and empower you as we all embark on the great adventure of this fabulous third act of our lives.

Tricia x.

Fabulous Makeup

Let's start with the quickest and easiest way to transform yourself and help you to feel and look better instantly – applying some gorgeous slap.

I have always loved makeup and I think it's true to say that I have applied it to my face every day for the past fifty years. You may think this sounds shallow, but for me applying my 'face' every morning is like breathing and is just as important as far as I am concerned. I also give thought to how my hair looks and what clothes and accessories I am going to wear. And I do all this whether I am going to meet other people or not. My rationale is simple: taking time and trouble over my appearance makes me feel more confident and more able to 'face the day'. It also gives me pleasure because I see it as an act of creativity, something I actively enjoy.

With makeup you can achieve a seriously professional effect in about twenty minutes if you know what you are doing and have the right tools and products. You can also make yourself look prettier, brighter, healthier and – yes – younger in the process. I want to persuade you that applying even a small amount of makeup can affect not only the way you look but also the way you feel about yourself and, as importantly in our ageist society, the way that others respond to you.

And yet, despite these considerable benefits, many women give up on makeup as they age. I dare say that some will think, 'Why bother?' If you fall into this category and I can't convince you otherwise, then feel free to skip to the next chapter. However, I know from experience that many older women love to wear makeup but sometimes feel overwhelmed and confused by the huge range of available products. Many are also fearful that wearing a full face of makeup might make them look ridiculous and inappropriate. They are told in articles in magazines by (usually young) beauty editors that 'less is more' when you are past the menopause. This utterly meaningless phrase seems to imply that makeup isn't safe for you any more. Better leave it to beautiful young girls with their smooth, flawless skin and perfectly applied feline, flicked, black-liquid eyeliner. I used to find that shopping for makeup was another age-related challenge. Beauty halls in department stores are uncomfortable and alien environments when you are older because there is absolutely nothing in them that reflects who you are. I have never looked at a twenty-something girl on a makeup counter and thought, 'I really want to look like you' – not because she doesn't look lovely but because she's twenty and I am forty years older. A friend found her experience of a makeover in a store so off-putting that she vowed never to wear makeup again!

Many older women love to wear make-up but feel overwhelmed by the huge range of available products.

Do Older Faces Need Makeup More Than Younger Ones?

I passionately believe that older faces actually need makeup *more* than younger ones. However, they don't need *more makeup* – just the right makeup applied in the right way. The reason I say this is down to some very interesting research on how people perceive and make assumptions about faces. One obvious assumption is how old the person appears to be. Most of you will no doubt be thinking that wrinkles and age spots are the main signifiers of ageing. However, the biggest difference between a young face and an older one is the loss of contrast between the features and the surrounding facial skin. As we get older we gradually lose melanin which results in a general 'fading', so that slowly but surely we have much less colour in our eyebrows, eye area, cheeks and lips. The brilliant news is that all this 'fading' can quickly and easily be corrected with makeup, so this is the primary benefit of applying colour cosmetics to your face. The secondary benefit is to even out the skin tone, cover blemishes, correct discolouration and add shape and luminosity to the face.

> **As we get older we gradually lose melanin which results in a general 'fading'.**

I know from experience that very many older women either give up on makeup or become increasingly less confident about how to apply it in order to look subtly enhanced. Maybe you are looking for some new ideas having become firmly stuck in a rut, or you just need a refresher to remind you of the best products to use and the best techniques to apply them, so let me guide you through some important considerations when it comes to your choice of makeup.

KIM
BEFORE

KIM
AFTER

MARY'S STORY

I NEVER LEARNED TO PUT ON MAKEUP AS A YOUNGSTER, and only very occasionally wore any since: I didn't think I needed it, lacked confidence in how to apply it, and thought, 'What's the point, I'll only be taking it off again in a few hours.'

Now in my later fifties, my hair is mostly white, my eyes are a mid-brown and my complexion much lighter. Then I swapped my glasses for contact lenses. Where my glasses had given my face definition and colour, there was now blandness. I seemed to disappear. I love my hair colour, it suits me, but you would never say I looked striking.

I started experimenting with makeup. I sat on a train and watched a young woman apply hers. What a routine, what a palaver! I Googled 'sparkly makeup for older women' and stumbled across one of Tricia's 'How to' videos. Here was a video that made complete sense, explaining what product to use and why. For the first time I understood what to do and what effect it would have. I also learned why my mascara looked heavy and messy, why my eyes didn't stand out, how to mitigate crepe-y eyelids, how to stop my lipstick bleeding into feathery lines, and many more important pointers and tips.

Just watching that first video gave me the confidence that even I could make myself up to look stunning. I watched more LFF videos and copied the look – each time I was pleased with the outcome and got fabulous feedback.

Now I *love* putting my makeup on. Yes, it takes time for my whole routine, but even then LFF has a 'Quick and Easy' video that's great if I'm in a rush. What utterly gorgeous products. I am so happy to have found Look Fabulous Forever. And so grateful to Tricia, Linda and all the models for showing me how to look, and feel, fabulous.

How, Why and Where to Apply Makeup to Your Face

First, think seriously about what your face makeup needs to achieve. If you have beautiful, clear, even skin, you may just need to brighten it with some blusher and highlighter, on top of a light covering of foundation. If your skin is blotchy with patches of discolouration then you will definitely need enough foundation to unify your skin tone so that it is the same colour all over. Then you will need concealer to camouflage any darker areas that are still visible after you have applied the base colour. Any really dark discolouration (either red or blue) can be further improved with colour correctors.

01 Always start with a clean, well-moisturised face. See pages 58–62 on Fabulous Skincare if you need help and guidance with this.

02 Make sure that your moisturiser has had time to be properly absorbed and don't apply your makeup immediately after a steamy shower or having blasted your hair with a hairdryer. If your face is hot, damp and flushed, you have created the perfect conditions to ensure that the makeup will immediately slide off!

03 Give yourself time to apply it properly. You may already be thinking, 'What an awful faff!', but if you get into the habit of devoting some care and attention to the process it will mean that, apart from refreshing your lipstick, you'll hardly have to glance at your face until bedtime because it will look perfect for hours.

04 Think of applying your 'face' as a creative and pleasurable daily pursuit. Just changing your attitude to the process turns it from 'chore' to 'cherishing'.

05 Make sure that you can see what you are doing! Bathrooms often have poor levels of natural light and the mirror may not be positioned to give you the best view. Combine that with failing eyesight and you'll have a recipe for disaster. The best solution is to look into a mirror while you are facing a large window, preferably in daylight.

06 Use a double-sided mirror (one side magnified and the other not) on a stand so that you can angle it as needed. Flip between both sides so that you can check that you have applied each product to best effect.

07 Attach a small, very magnifying mirror (up to ten times magnification) to a larger plain mirror to ensure you have no stray hairy horrors around the mouth, chin or elsewhere. It can also help to check that eye makeup doesn't look messy.

I'VE ALWAYS LOVED MAKEUP. I remember being chosen, aged ten, to play Mary in the school nativity; not for my natural acting ability, but because I was taller than any of the other girls. I was thrilled to be wearing lipstick for the performance and was devastated when it had to be washed off at bedtime.

Having spent most of my career in corporate sales in the IT and telecoms arenas, I decided to call it a day when aged fifty-eight. I realised that the stress of the job was making me increasingly miserable. It seemed to me that I had reached an age when I should be able to choose what I wanted to do. So I enrolled at the London School of Beauty and Make-up and joined a class of women, the oldest of whom was thirty-two, on a full-time course. I passed my exams with flying colours and launched myself upon an unsuspecting industry.

A stroke of pure luck gave me the opportunity to do the makeup for a fashion show at the V&A museum in London where, after the show, two of the other makeup artists asked if I would model for them at a fashion shoot for their degree course. Emboldened by my new 'carpe diem' attitude, I said yes and a (very late) modelling career was born! Since then, I've done lots of photo shoots and TV appearances and have been made up by many, almost exclusively young, makeup artists.

Most of them are very skilful, but only a handful have any idea how to make up the face of a woman in her sixties. I've been given Cara Delevingne brows (horrendous on me), contoured, highlighted, covered with thick, heavy foundation and generally made to look not only ridiculous, but at least ten years older. I had a little epiphany and decided to specialise in makeup for older women.

It has turned out to be the most joyful and rewarding decision I've ever made. We women, including the models I work with, all have a host of insecurities no matter how confident we look on the outside. I often hear from the women sitting in my makeup chair that they feel washed out, invisible, intimidated by the whole idea of putting makeup on; that they are not sure it's worth it. It's incredibly satisfying when someone comes to me for a makeup lesson and can't believe the difference properly applied concealer under the eyes makes, or how the right blusher applied in the right place brings her whole face to life.

I've been working with Tricia and Look Fabulous Forever since pretty much the very beginning. I love the fact that we work with real women with real imperfections and I'm always as delighted as they are by the results we achieve with the LFF products. We don't airbrush, we don't use special lighting, we just use the power of makeup and it works wonders.

How to Apply Beautiful Face Makeup

Step One

/

START WITH PRIMER

Many older women are unfamiliar with face primers, but they are a brilliant way to help your makeup look instantly better. A primer is also an essential item if you are going to have a long day and you want your makeup to look as immaculate at bedtime as it did when you applied it first thing in the morning. A tall order but it's perfectly possible with primers.

A face primer has the effect of smoothing the skin and making it less absorbent so that your makeup will last longer. One of the biggest problems of post-menopausal skin is that it is thirsty and highly absorbent. I use the analogy of blotting paper to explain the problem of getting makeup to stay put for any length of time. Contrast the way that blotting paper performs with normal paper. The latter is smooth and shiny and feels delightful to the touch; it is also possible to draw a line on it with ink and the line will be sharp and crisp. Now think about the feel of blotting paper. It is much rougher to the touch and has no shine, but it has a dense texture and is very absorbent. So when I came up with the idea for a makeup range specifically formulated for older skin, I knew that I wanted to have a great primer for the face, to overcome the 'blotting paper' problem of makeup that disappears and may look messy.

• **How to apply a face primer:** There are two ways you can do this. Remember that it goes on top of your moisturiser and, when applied and dry, the skin should feel as smooth as satin. So, either put a pea-sized amount on the back of your hand and then lightly spread it over the whole face, or if you are in a hurry, then mix the face primer with your foundation and apply like that. It will still work just as well at keeping your makeup in place for hours.

Step Two

/

UNIFY YOUR SKIN TONE

Foundation is just like a good bra! It makes everything you put on top look better. Many women tell me they only use a tinted moisturiser and I invariably think, 'I wish I could quickly apply some foundation to show you how much better your face would look if your skin tone looked more even.' Foundation needs to cover well without looking like a thick, dull, caked-on mask. I think it's the fear of this effect that puts a lot of older women off. But modern liquid foundations are quite miraculous. They work best when applied with a foundation brush which you use to 'buff' the product into the skin. Start in the centre of the face and work outwards so that the foundation is most lightly applied at the hair and jawlines. Match it to the colour of the skin at your jaw and smooth over the jawline so that it fades out towards your neck. That way your face will be a similar colour to your neck and will not appear to be 'floating' above it.

Step Three

/

CONTINUE THE GOOD WORK WITH CONCEALERS & COLOUR CORRECTORS

Now use a small stiff brush to stipple a dense and creamy concealer to cover any areas you feel need some extra help. The colour of the concealer should be as close as possible to your foundation as it needs to blend perfectly. I use a concealer daily in that blue hollow bit in the inner corners of my eyes, in the under-eye area and also on individual spots which may be in my T-zone. I then use the warmth of my finger to pat the product into the skin so that it stays put. Another good trick is to dot some lightweight translucent powder on top of the concealer. Also, if you have any redness across your nose or cheeks, you can neutralise it with a green colour corrector, while blueness can be balanced with a peachy-toned corrector.

Step Four

/

THINK SHAPE, COLOUR & LUMINESCENCE

This is where the fun starts! Use a highlighter to add a touch of subtle shimmer to your brow bones and also to the top of your cheekbones. Highlighters can also be used down the centre of the nose to make it look thinner and around the mouth to help lipstick colour to 'pop'. Ideally, a highlighter should not be noticeable except where it catches the light. Apply with the integrated brush and pat into the skin with your fingers.

Step Five

/

BLUSHER

An essential item in your makeup bag. The moment you apply a beautiful pinky or peach-toned blusher is the moment that the whole face comes to life. I prefer blushers in a cream-to-powder formulation because they create a smoother effect on an older face. Powder blushers tend to sit in any wrinkles on your cheeks, while cream blushers are often too lightweight. We are often told to apply blusher to the 'apples' of the cheeks, but I feel this is misleading. So start at the centre of the eye and go down until you can feel the cheekbone. Use your fingers or a brush to apply the blusher as an arc rather than a circle of colour onto the cheekbone, sweeping it out and up towards the top of the ears. Blend really well with a fat brush so that there are no hard edges.

Step Six (*optional*)

/

POWDERS & BRONZERS

For special occasions, especially if you will have your photograph taken, add a light dusting of translucent powder over your completed *maquillage*. Somehow it just makes your look more 'finished'. In the summer, a lovely light swirl of bronzer can create a delightful 'sun-kissed' appearance to the face in the prettiest way.

NOW FOR EYE MAKEUP

We forget that before the Sixties, eye makeup was rudimentary and few women wore much more than a touch of mascara on their eyes. And even that was a very basic item. Do you remember mascara in small rectangular compacts in solid blocks of colour that you wet with spit (yuk) and rubbed with a stubby little brush and then applied to the lashes? Not the most hygienic or the most glamorous product! Photographs of Marilyn Monroe in the Fifties show her with beautiful full red lips, but little in the way of eye makeup apart from groomed eyebrows and a touch of mascara. Widely available mass-produced and inexpensive eye makeup came of age as we did in the 1960s. Remember Elizabeth Taylor's dramatic eye makeup as Cleopatra and that iconic photo of Twiggy in the mid-Sixties with her huge and heavily made-up doe eyes, each lower lash painstakingly painted on individually? I was eighteen in 1966 and very well recall the excitement of buying Mary Quant's wonderfully fresh and inventive range of eye makeup, with her trademark daisy logo, called things like 'Jeepers Peepers' and 'Bring Back the Lash' mascara which you applied with a wand. Mary Quant also changed the way that makeup was sold. The idea was to create a fun 'art shop' environment where you could play with the colours, which was a million miles from the stuffy atmosphere of the traditional beauty halls.

> **Widely available mass-produced and inexpensive eye makeup came of age as we did in the 1960s.**

The Importance of Eye Makeup on an Older Face

Eye makeup is probably the most challenging aspect of makeup for the majority of older women. We came of age wearing a lot of the black stuff around our eyes with deathly pale lips and we loved the way it made us look sultry and smouldering like Brigitte Bardot (we wished!), or arty and intellectual like Juliette Gréco. Above all, we didn't want to look remotely like our mothers with their 'powdered noses' and matte red lips.

Now we are older ourselves, many of us shy away from applying eye makeup for fear of looking like some tragic old pantomime dame desperately clinging onto our youth. The only real dame who pulls off the trick of looking good with heavily made-up black-rimmed eyes and lashings of volumising mascara on top of false eyelashes is Joan Collins, but she is a force of nature and is above reproof. The other dame who comes to mind is Barbara Cartland, the romantic novelist, who also went for rather less successful dramatic eye makeup in her eighties.

Best Approaches to Eye Makeup When You Are Older

So let's look at the best approaches to eye makeup when the ageing process has changed the shape of our eyes, the texture of the skin of our eyelids, and the quality and thickness of our eyelashes and eyebrows.

Step One

/

GET YOUR EYEBROWS SORTED

This is the very best tip I can give you, if you want not only your eyes, but also your whole face to look instantly more attractive. We like looking at faces which are symmetrical. Eyebrows play an important role in creating that proportion and symmetry. Tracey, a breast cancer survivor, told me recently that when chemo robbed her of her brows it made her look permanently startled and frightened, which was how she felt inside. Very scant, faded or non-existent brows unbalance the face, so restoring subtle definition is vital.

If your eyebrows are like mine and have become wiry and rather overgrown, straggly and shapeless, then I suggest you go to a salon and get them threaded into a good neat shape. You can then maintain that shape if you tidy them regularly (back to the ten-times magnifying mirror!). Now you are ready to add some definition to your brows.

I devised the LFF Brow Shape for a close relative, Jenny, whose eyebrows had fallen out due to a thyroid deficiency. Using the Brow Shape, you can create a very natural-looking and subtle effect indistinguishable from real eyebrows. Think of yourself creating eyebrows on a portrait as an artist, using light, feathery strokes of colour to simulate the individual hairs, rather than drawing on two approximations of eyebrows as if you were a child. Eyebrows should be sisters not twins and need to be the same width apart as the base of your nose. Measure this with a pencil and then place at an angle from the base of the nose across to the outer corner of the eye, you will see where the eyebrow should end.

Step Two

/

PREPARE YOUR EYELIDS

One of the biggest problems with older eyelids is that eye makeup doesn't stay put. I often see my contemporaries with messy, ragged black lines around their eyes because they have tried to replicate the solid neat black lines which young women achieve on their perfectly smooth, wrinkle-free eyelids with liquid or gel liners. Fortunately, you can easily improve the look of eye makeup on a thinner, crepe-y eyelid by applying a flesh-coloured eye primer. This will smooth the skin and neutralise any discolouration there may be. I apply a very fine layer of eye primer to my eyelid every day with a similar brush to the one I use for concealer.

Step Three

/

EYE SHADOW

Using this can reshape the eyes in quite dramatic ways. My eyes used to be almond shaped but are now smaller and more round. I preferred them the way they were, so I use eye makeup to restore their former shape and size as much as I can. Start by assessing your eyes in a mirror. Look at the shape and size of your eyes and how they are set into the eye socket. Hooded eyes will have no discernible socket line, while deep-set eyes will have a very dark and defined socket line. Maybe your lashes are sparse and short at the top and practically non-existent on the bottom lid. If you are lucky there will be three clearly defined areas: a brow bone, a socket line and an eyelid. The whole eye is framed at the top by the brow and at the bottom by the lower lashes.

• **Types of eye shadows:** My suggestion is that you always use completely matte eye shadows which will add colour and shading without drawing attention to the creases on your lids, unlike frosted or shimmery shadows. I also suggest that you start with very soft, pale colours in neutral tones like grey, cream and taupe. The simplest eye makeup you can do is to apply a pale eye shadow to the lid and then take a complementary darker shadow and apply a very fine line of this colour to the lash line using a small wedge-shaped brush. For instance, I would team cream with cocoa brown, pale grey with charcoal grey, taupe with dark green or dark purple. Don't aim for perfection, just push the darker shade into the base of the lashes with the brush and sweep the colour up and away at the outer edge. You could leave it there or take a mid-tone colour and add some shading into the socket line. Then blend all three shadows with a clean eye shadow brush to create a pretty, slightly smoky effect. I also apply a soft line of shadow along my lower eyelashes too. However, this needs to be done smudgily rather than as a solid jet-black line.

• **Adding some brightness:** If you feel that the matte shadows look rather dull, especially for an evening look, then use a slightly shiny cream smoother like the LFF Lid Colour. These can be used across the whole lid or just the inner third of the eyelid in a colour to enhance your eyes. I apply them after I've applied shadow to the socket line with a small stiff brush.

Step Four

/

EYELASH CURLERS

All eyelashes, however sparse, can be improved with both eyelash curlers and mascara. Eyelash curlers take practice but once you have mastered them, they really can make a world of difference to how open and pretty your eyes appear. Look straight ahead into a magnifying mirror. Open the curlers and trap as much of your lashes as you can without catching the skin on your eyelid. As this is painful you will know immediately if you are squeezing part of the lid. Now close the curlers and pump around ten times. If your lashes are long enough you can pull the curlers up slightly and pump again further up the lashes to complete the effect. Always use the curlers on clean lashes and apply the mascara afterwards, otherwise it will clump the lashes together.

Step Five

/

MASCARA

If you can only be bothered to apply one item of eye makeup, then choose mascara! Nothing makes such an instant improvement to the look of your eyes – assuming you have shaped and made up your brows first. I dislike mascaras that have lengthening and volumising filaments in them.

It would seem logical to apply as much thickening mascara as you can, but this creates a rather hard, spiky effect which, paradoxically, makes the lashes look even more sparse – much better to darken and define them but leave the lashes silky and pliable to the touch. That way they will look natural and soft while making your eyes look bigger and prettier.

SMOKY EYES

If you like the idea of a sultry, smoky eye, then go for it, but steer clear of loading on a very dark colour over the whole lid or you'll look like the mother in the Addams Family! *Here's how:*

1/ Groom and define your brows. Very pale brows and very heavy eye shadow is not a good look!

2/ Choose three eye shadows that work together. For cool tones try pale grey, taupe and charcoal or aubergine. For warm tones choose cream, taupe and cocoa brown or forest green.

3/ Apply the palest colour of shadow over the whole eyelid and a mid-tone to the socket line.

4/ Using a small wedge brush take the darkest colour and apply it to the lash line and outer third of the eyelid. You can also take a small amount under the bottom lash line too. Blend really well.

5/ Add two or three coats of mascara to curled eyelashes, top and bottom.

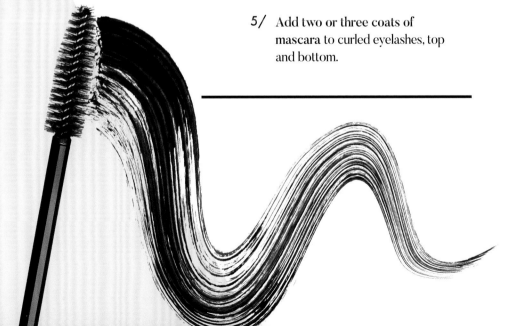

Challenges with Eye Makeup

WEARING SPECS

The most common problem is failing eyesight and the need to wear glasses either all the time or in order to be able to apply your makeup. I can't solve the poor eyesight problem, but would urge you to discuss possible solutions with your optician. You can buy glasses which flip up on alternate sides so that you can see through one lens while the other is flipped up for application to that eye and vice versa. Magnifying mirrors may well be a good solution or contact lenses just for makeup application. If you really cannot solve this problem then get your eyebrows looking as good as possible because they will be very noticeable above your glasses. Then apply mascara if you possibly can. Keep the eye makeup to a minimum and concentrate on unifying your skin tone, adding a blusher and a really flattering lipstick. That way you will look pretty and groomed without having to worry about eye makeup.

Best Eye Makeup with Specs: My Top Tips

◆ Keep it light and minimal. Choose paler neutral colours as anything darker will look overdone.

◆ Make sure that you define the lash line but choose a shadow in a purple, dark green or cocoa brown rather than black so that eyelashes look as thick as possible.

◆ When you apply eye shadow colours think about matching or toning with your frames. I saw a friend recently and she looked fabulous with her short spiky white hair, dark purple frames and grey eye shadow. She was also wearing a vibrant lipstick in a cherry-red colour for a real wow factor.

◆ Use eyelash curlers to keep your lashes from touching the lenses of your glasses and choose a waterproof mascara which should stay put better. Be aware that the glasses may magnify any dark under-eye circles, so apply concealer over a colour corrector to ensure the skin matches the rest of your face.

HOODED EYES OR DEEP-SET EYES

I am not going to call these 'problems' so much as 'differences'. Charlotte Rampling has trademark hooded eyes with no discernible socket line and she has always been seen as seriously sultry and alluring. If you want to apply makeup to your own hooded eyes to make them look bigger, you can use a lighter shadow on the eyelid (you may have to lift the loose skin which has descended over part of the lid) and then create the illusion of a socket line with a slightly darker toning shadow, then blend well. Well-shaped eyebrows, a highlighter on the brow bone and a couple of coats of mascara will complete the look.

Deep-set eyes Like those of Daphne Selfe (left) can look rather sunken so compensate by lightening the naturally darkly shadowed socket line. Pay particular attention to the inner corners of the eyes and apply a creamy concealer. Now use a lighter shadow over the entire lid, including the socket line. The eyelids are likely to be a good size, so darken the lash line with shadow and use this to darken the outer third of the eyelid. Finish with mascara on both the top and bottom lashes.

ANGIE

Lips

Lipstick and mascara would be my desert island essentials, along with a pillow so I could sleep comfortably. Obviously, the lippy could double as a blusher, but I also see lipstick as the most fabulous way to look instantly better and brighter for when my rescuers arrive. I adore red lips on older women. There is something about the combination of silvery white hair and red lips that is alluring in the best possible way. And yet I get quite a number of antagonistic remarks on my Facebook page when I am wearing a dark cherry-red lip colour. 'Older women shouldn't wear red lipstick' is the comment I frequently receive, and I feel like saying, 'In your opinion, but not mine!' If like me you love a bright and vibrant slash of colour, then I'd say, 'Go for it!' Just make sure that the shade works with your skin tone. A blue-red for cool tones and an orangey-red for warm tones.

> **There is something about the combination of silvery white hair and red lips that is alluring in the best possible way.**

Lips become thinner and paler with age so the purpose of lip makeup is to make them look more full and luscious. I have a problem with my lip colour migrating over the edges and feathering into the lines around my mouth. A lip primer will stop this in its tracks and allow you to create a clean, sharp line. Apply the primer to the edges only, as it isn't a balm; nor is it intended to moisturise the lips. I personally dislike lip liners because I hate that look of the line that gets left as lipstick wears off. I realise you might not feel the same but please remember that a liner should match your natural lip colour as opposed to your lipstick.

To make the colour of your lippy last longer, try this four-step process:

1 Apply a coat of lipstick and rub the colour into your lips with your finger to create a stain.

2 Using a brush carefully apply one coat. By pressing just above the edge of the lips you can create your own 'trout pout' and this will allow you to apply the lipstick to the maximum area of lip.

3 Blot your lips with a tissue and apply a final coat.

4 Top with a small amount of clear lip gloss by dabbing it lightly on top to make lips looks as full as possible. This also looks more fabulous for evenings out.

Choosing Colours

Do you know which are the most flattering colours to wear both next to and on your face? Many years ago the must-have fashionable colours for that season were shades of brown, so, in order to be 'with it', I bought a brown-orange lipstick. I wore it a couple of times but always felt unhappy with the way I looked without having a clue why. At the time, I had no idea that there are certain colours which work against your natural skin tone in the worst possible way. In theory, we should all be able to wear whatever colour we want, but in practice it helps enormously to know whether the undertone of your skin is blue or yellow. Mine is blue or cool, so the fashionable lipstick I bought was completely wrong and the reason it did not suit me. So if you wear the colours that work best with your skin tone, both in makeup and what you wear near your face, you will instantly look brighter, healthier and more 'glowing'.

> **In theory, we should all be able to wear whatever colour we want, but it helps to know whether the undertone of your skin is blue or yellow.**

I think the confusion happens because we think that eye and hair colour are the best indicators of the makeup choices we need to make. This may or may not be true. My daughter Anna is a brown-eyed redhead with the kind of skin that rarely tans. My other daughter Suzy is a green-eyed blonde and her skin tans very easily. Despite these differences, they both look best in makeup colours like brown, peach, coral, orange, green and caramel. However (and this is where it gets confusing), when it comes to clothes Anna looks better in strong and quite vibrant warm colours (autumn), while Suzy suits softer, less vibrant warm shades (spring). Neither looks their best in black, which tends to

45 /

ZENA
warm
tones

make a warm-toned skin look very washed-out, but needless to say, like many warm-toned women they both often choose to wear it! I am very cool-toned (winter), which means that the undertone of my skin is blue not yellow. When I was younger my hair was mid-brown and my eyes are grey. Now my hair is going grey and I have white highlights added at the front. That orangey-brown lipstick was a disaster on me because I really cannot wear colours on my face that have any trace of yellow in them. For eye colours I look my best in taupe, grey, charcoal and aubergine, and a rose pink is a good choice for cheek colour. On my lips, I have to wear pinky, plummy, cherry shades – pinks or reds with a blue base rather than anything brown or orange.

To make it even more complicated there are women who can wear either cool or warm tones on and next to their skin. It is quite unusual but it does happen. If you are neutral you will find it almost impossible to decide one way or the other (warm or cool) because you may look equally good in, say, orange and fuchsia.

HOW TO DECIDE IF YOU'RE WARM OR COOL TONED

01 Take off all your makeup and use a mirror, preferably in good natural light. Place different-coloured scarves or tops under your chin and evaluate the effect. If you are still unsure, ask someone to help you to decide which ones make you look better.

02 Try just applying a lipstick with no other makeup. Choose one that is a warm orangey-brown and one that is a cool pinky-red. Again, appraise the effect in a good light. It should be fairly obvious which looks better.

03 Do you wear gold or silver jewellery? Gold tends to look more flattering against warm-toned skin and silver next to cool-toned skin.

04 Don't be confused by white or grey hair. White and grey are cool tones, right? Yes. However, if you have a warm skin tone and your hair goes white, your makeup still needs to be warm-toned. See Zena and the makeup she is wearing – a good example of a white-haired person with warm-toned skin. Zena's soft-brown blouse and gold necklace work perfectly with her skin tone.

05 If you receive compliments when you wear a particular outfit, notice which colours get the most plaudits. When we get it right (no mustard yellow for me!), people notice that you look nice and will say so.

06 And a final word about foundation colours. It's important to match your foundation colour to your jawline so that the face doesn't appear to be 'floating above' your neck. As a general rule, apart from alabaster white skin (which is very rare), steer clear of pinky-toned foundation. Whether cool or warm, foundations with a yellow base look much more flattering than pink ones on most skin tones. Add extra warmth in the summer with a light dusting of bronzer on top of foundation for a sun-kissed glow.

The Best Tools for Applying Makeup

You may well use your fingers to apply your face makeup or make do with those little brushes or foam-topped applicators that are sometimes included with blushers, concealers and eye shadows. If you employed a decorator to paint a room in your house, would you be happy if he or she started to spread the paint with their fingers? And if they did you'd probably not be too surprised if the walls or woodwork ended up looking a bit patchy and lumpy. So my best suggestion is that you become your own makeup artist and that you equip yourself with the right tools for the job.

1/

Foundation brushes need to be big and full enough to buff liquid foundation into your face. Put the product onto the back of your hand and swirl the brush around to distribute it evenly throughout the brush. Then continue to use a swirling movement to spread the base over the face.

to 'fade' the base towards the hairline and over the jawline and ensure that the foundation isn't sitting on top of my skin but is fully integrated with it. Also useful to sweep a fine covering of translucent powder to reduce shine and set your makeup, and you can apply light touches of bronzer with this brush wherever the sun kisses your face.

2/

Powder brushes are the fattest of all and I love these to 'polish' my face after I have applied the base. I keep a clean one just for this purpose and it works perfectly

3/

Concealer brushes need to be quite short and stubby so that you can 'stipple' the creamy concealer into the skin. I also use a very fine small brush to 'dot'

concealer onto small individual spots – voila! They magically disappear.

4 /

Blusher brushes need to be soft and plump so that you can blend the colour thoroughly by sweeping it in a pretty arc across the cheeks.

5 /

Eye shadow brushes: You will need a few small, soft brushes to apply eye shadow. I use a minimum of three. One for applying paler colours, one for darker colours and one I keep clean for blending. Brushes are much better than the little foam-topped applicators that come with many eye shadows.

6 /

A small wedge-shaped brush allows me to create a lash line quickly and precisely.

7 /

A spoolie brush is great for grooming eyebrows both before and after you have added colour.

8 /

Eyelash curlers are a great addition to your toolkit. I use mine every day.

Makeup Routines

/

QUICK & EASY

If you only have five minutes you can still significantly improve your look. Just add the right kind of colour and definition to a face that has been thoroughly moisturised:

1   Apply your foundation to unify skin tone.

2   Add a sweep of blusher to brighten the face.

3   Define your brows to create balance and proportion.

4   Add a coat of mascara to make eyes bigger and more open.

5   Apply a lipstick to add a pretty final touch.

Routine Two

/

SPECIAL OCCASIONS

There are certain times when we really want to ramp up the glamour. I well remember being the mother of the bride for my two daughters and being determined to look my absolute best. After all, you are the second most important female at the wedding and those wedding photographs are going to be around for a long time as the only tangible memory of the day. I wanted to have no regrets when I looked at the photos, rather than an appalled 'what on earth was I thinking?' I also went to a similar amount of trouble in preparation for my sixtieth birthday, which was an evening party with a large group of my friends.

> **For my special events, I had a few facials at a local beauty salon to improve the texture of my skin.**

If you have a special occasion coming up, it's a very good idea to start your preparation for extra fabulousness two to three months before the event. This will allow you to follow a comprehensive skincare regime and ensure that the canvas onto which the makeup will be applied is in the best condition possible. For my special events, I had a few facials at a local beauty salon to improve the texture of my skin, and I also had a course of CACI treatments. These stimulate the circulation of blood to the face and also tighten the muscles to perceptibly reduce sagging. These treatments weren't cheap but were definitely worth the investment. If your budget is limited then you can achieve good results at home if you plan a regime of regular attention with exfoliators and face masks.

TOP TIPS

for SPECIAL OCCASIONS

01 First decide on your outfit.

02 Practise your makeup before the day and make notes to remind yourself if necessary. Try new things if you feel like it, but do get feedback from a trusted friend if you are not sure. Make a list of everything you will need to pack if you won't be getting ready at home.

03 Experiment with colours on your eyes and lips while wearing your outfit. Keep eye makeup colours neutral if you are going for a vibrant lip colour.

04 Pack a mirror on a stand and position it so that you are facing a window in full daylight. Hotel bathrooms are usually dreadful places to put makeup on as they have no natural light.

05 Wear a face primer. This is essential to help your makeup look smooth and last for hours regardless of heat, people kissing you, dancing and tears.

06 Use brushes to apply everything and blend, blend, blend, especially at the jawline, hairline and on the eyes.

07 Don't overload the makeup. Face, eye and lip primers will help everything to stay put. In evening light you may need to apply a touch more blusher and maybe a stronger lip colour.

08 Use concealer for any discolouration including under-eye circles, age spots and in the inner corner of the eyes. This will really help your skin look flawless in photographs.

Routine Three

/

WEDDINGS

Weddings are usually daytime affairs and so your makeup needs to look good in natural light. Because of this, I'd go for a soft and pretty look rather than ramped-up glamour. Aim for something which enhances and complements your overall outfit so that you look stylish and groomed from top to toe. Makeup colours need to tone with your clothes, especially your lipstick. For instance, if you have chosen an ice-blue outfit and you have fair or grey hair then choose a cool-toned pink lipstick – by which I mean one with a blue undertone. However, if you choose cream, beige or brown, which are all warm-toned, then pink will only work if you have a cool skin tone. See more under 'Choosing Colours' (page 44).

On the day of the wedding: You may be needed to provide lots of help and support for the bride or groom, so I suggest you get your hair dressed early in the day. Then you won't be applying your makeup in steamy conditions to a damp, flushed face having just blasted your hair with heat. Leave at least 45 minutes to do your face, so that you aren't desperately slapping your makeup on just before the ceremony.

Routine Four

/

CRUISES

Cruises are a wonderful opportunity to have some fun with your make-up. You are on holiday, maybe in the sun, so you will need to adjust your look to accommodate a (slight) tan and a very different light. I spend a good part of the summer in the southern half of France where the light is Mediterranean, so I know that the makeup I have loved throughout a UK winter will no longer cut the mustard. I have never put my face in the sun, so for years I have used a fake tan to ensure that my face is a similar colour to my neck and décolletage.

To apply fake tan:

1 | Ensure that the skin is clean and exfoliated as tan will 'grab' any dry patches.

2 | I prefer a white cream to a coloured cream as it doesn't stain the bedding!

3 | Spread as evenly as you can over the face in a light covering. Rub it thoroughly into the skin.

4 | Now wet a cotton pad and add some soap. Go round the edges of the hairline with the pad to remove any excess fake tan that has accumulated there.

5 | The next morning wash your face with a face cloth which will soften the effect to look more natural.

Routine Five

/

SUMMER SUNSHINE

With the fake tan you probably won't need a foundation, so apply a tinted moisturiser. I tend to use a light covering of foundation because my skin needs it, so I mix bronze-coloured tint with my normal foundation to darken it slightly. This saves me having to buy another base and I can add more tint as needed. Keep your eye makeup light by using soft, neutral colours and make sure that you apply a lovely peachy or pink-toned blusher. Bronzer can look wonderful swept over the forehead, with light touches to the cheeks and chin – you are adding it wherever the sun might hit your face. I also find that a very bright lipstick works brilliantly on a summer face when the light is brighter and stronger than in the grey light of winter.

Fabulous Skincare

My skin has good bits and bad bits. The good bits are the relative lack of wrinkles which is most likely due to my genetic inheritance, which is pure chance, and also to the fact that I don't drink alcohol or smoke, which is a lifestyle choice. The bad bit of my skin is the acne rosacea from which I suffer. After puberty I had occasional outbreaks of acne on my face, chest and back. These seemed to be related to my hormones and diet. Since the menopause I have developed a form of acne rosacea, with the acne part being more problematic. In other words, I frequently get painful lumps and spots around my nose, chin and forehead. There are many days when I look in my mirror with quiet despair at my very patchy, spotty skin. Fortunately, once I have put on my face makeup really carefully with judiciously applied concealer, I am ready to face the day knowing that few people will guess just how bad my skin actually looks.

IMPROVING THE TEXTURE OF YOUR SKIN

There are many ways that older skin can be improved with a little effort and know-how. Skin has three layers. The surface, which people see when they look at your face is the epidermis. This will show all the effects of 'lifestyle' damage and can be significantly improved by good skincare. The epidermis is held up by a scaffold of protein fibres in a layer known as the dermis. This structure changes as we age, especially as oestrogen levels drop with the menopause, and those changes cause all the hallmarks of visually older-looking skin, including wrinkling, sagging and age spots. The dermis is much harder to change regardless of how many 'anti-ageing' potions you apply. The third layer is the hypodermis and has the veins, nerves and blood vessels which are also essential to the health of your skin.

The easiest layer of skin to get to is obviously the outer one. Keeping the epidermis clean, exfoliated and moisturised can have a dramatic effect on how you look and how well your makeup performs when applied to your face. Because the beauty industry is so obsessed with youthful ageing, it also wants you to believe that lotions and potions can penetrate to the dermis and affect the density of the collagen and elastin and thereby slow the natural ageing process. They can't. The problem is that the epidermis is designed to create a very effective protective barrier to the dermis, so topically applied lotions and potions will improve the surface, but they will not structurally alter the dermis.

QUICKEST WAYS TO DAMAGE YOUR SKIN:

1/ **Sunbathing:** Some dermatologists believe that up to 80 per cent of ageing in white skin is caused by sun damage. The message is clear: use sunscreen on your face all year round. I currently use a moisturiser on my face and neck every day with an SPF of 30.

2/ **Smoking:** Nicotine reduces blood flow to the dermis as well as antioxidants like vitamin C, a key component in collagen production. Smoking also produces free radicals and enzymes which destroy collagen. A smoker's skin often looks ten years older than its chronological age.

3/ **Alcohol:** This impairs the absorption of vitamins A, D and E. It dehydrates the skin and dilates the blood vessels to make the face look red and puffy.

4/ **Diet:** Constant dieting can cause wrinkling of the skin and create a gaunt look. Japanese women often look several years younger than their western counterparts because their diet is rich in oily fish and vegetables.

BEST WAYS

to IMPROVE YOUR SKIN

1/

Sleep: It's not called 'beauty sleep' for nothing! I've mentioned how alcohol can disturb the quality of your rest at night, but so can caffeine, eating a late heavy meal, variable bedtime routines and the amount of exercise you get. I find relaxation techniques are also helpful for those times when 'something on your mind' leads to poor quality sleep.

2/

Exercise: Advantageous in so many ways, increased exercise will also benefit your skin because increased blood flow and circulation nourishes skin cells. I also find exercise helps to lower my stress levels.

3/

Cleansing: Every day our faces are assaulted by a cocktail of dirt and grime from polluted air. If, like me, you apply makeup every day then it has to be removed effectively. Please invest in a proper creamy cleanser rather than grabbing a pack of wipes. These are great in an emergency (and can be a good temporary back-up in hospital) but are not thorough enough for daily skin cleansing. Apply the cleanser liberally and then rinse off with a clean flannel doused in warm water. Keep a stock of flannels for the purpose and wash them daily.

4 /

Moisturising: Attracting and holding moisture in the skin is the quickest way to make skin look brighter, healthier and plumper. Apply moisturiser liberally over the whole face and neck twice a day. I like to apply a serum first and then add another layer of moisture with a day cream. See overleaf for beneficial ingredients in serums and day and night creams.

5 /

Exfoliation: Regularly ridding the epidermis of surface dead skin cells is an instant brightener. Best to go carefully if skin is sensitive or you suffer from conditions like psoriasis, eczema or, like me, acne rosacea. Always take advice from your doctor or dermatologist, especially if you experience any redness, itching or flaking.

6 /

Sunscreens: Look for moisturisers that incorporate a high level of SPF and then you can rest assured that your skin is protected (as long as you have a very thorough daily skincare regime). Even in winter, the moisturiser will be protecting you from UVA and UVB damage. Every layer you add to your skin adds a protective effect.

7 /

Diet and liquid intake: Eating a diet rich in antioxidants, vitamins and minerals and good fats (olive oil, oily fish, avocados and nuts) combined with sufficient water will nourish and hydrate the skin. More of this in the section on Fabulous Foods (page 202–9).

INGREDIENTS TO LOOK FOR
IN SKINCARE PREPARATIONS

There are some proven benefits to the skin from certain
ingredients, so look for mention of these on labels and jars.

◆ Hyaluronic acid:
This occurs naturally in the body and can significantly increase hydration. Its unique property is that it acts like a sponge, attracting and holding water in the skin, which in turn makes the skin look firmer and more luminous. It also works to keep skin more supple, reduces the appearance of fine lines and wrinkles, and improves the texture of the skin. Look for products which list sodium hyaluronate, hydrolysed acid, sodium acetyl hyaluronate and, of course, hyaluronic acid.

◆ Alpha hydroxy acids:
AHAs are mostly derived from plant sources. For example, citric acid comes from lemons and oranges, glycolic acid from sugar cane, lactic acid from milk, malic acid from apples, pyruvic acid from papayas and tartaric acid from grapes. So they are a natural way to exfoliate dead skin cells from the surface of the skin. Get rid of these and the skin looks brighter and feels smoother. However, a word of caution: AHAs make skin extra-sensitive to the sun and may cause redness and irritation. Look for concentrations of around 3 per cent if you have sensitive skin and use no more than once a week.

◆ Retinol:
This is a form of vitamin A and studies show that over a period of several months retinol products may have an impact on wrinkles, open pores, uneven skin tone and age spots. Retinol may initially cause redness and flaking (especially if at prescription strength), but this should diminish after a week or so. Retinol creams also need to be used in conjunction with a broad-spectrum sunblock to prevent sun damage.

Cosmetic Procedures

I hope you didn't buy this book expecting to get guidance on the best invasive cosmetic procedures for your ageing face. I do understand the temptation if you feel unhappy when you look in the mirror, but I believe that this dissatisfaction is caused by the anti-ageing rhetoric of the beauty industry, which seeks to persuade us that the only acceptable way to age is by doing all we can to look as young as possible. I would never condemn anyone who chose a facelift, Botox, dermal fillers or any other promise of instant rejuvenation; however I just don't buy that solution personally because I don't buy the problem. If you do decide that you want to have some form of 'work' done to your face, then let me offer a couple of words of caution. Firstly, remember that, once started, you will be committing to regular costly procedures which may make your face look progressively more weird rather than youthful. And secondly, this is not a well-regulated industry, so please do your homework and get the very best advice and therapies from well-qualified and experienced practitioners.

The main reason that I am so sceptical about invasive cosmetic interventions is because there are much quicker, cheaper and easier ways to look better, healthier and more fabulous than resorting to the knife, the needle and the laser. This book is full of such ideas and they have few risks attached. Do you remember the TV programme which promised that the volunteers would look 'ten years younger'? Participants were given a variety of cosmetic treatments, and then restyled with a top-to-toe makeover. In my opinion it was the beautiful makeup, smart haircut and fashionable new clothes that really transformed the way that the women looked for the final reveal to friends and family. That is why I don't think you need a facelift to look fabulous. Simply follow the ideas in these chapters on transforming your makeup, hair and style, and wait for the compliments!

Fabulous
Style

In the past I really enjoyed the process of buying something new to wear.

By which I mean the excitement of taking something into a changing room, liking it enough to buy it and then trying the item on at home to see how well it works with other clothes in my wardrobe. Sometimes this has led to disillusionment and a decision to take the item back, and sometimes it has ended in real delight as the garment proves to be the perfect addition to create a fabulous outfit. However, as I have aged it has become more and more difficult to find clothes that satisfy my desire to look stylish but age-appropriate. I accept that the term 'age-appropriate' is decried by many older women who believe that we can, and should, wear whatever we want. I wouldn't disagree, but I have a horror of being labelled 'mutton dressed as lamb', and also have no desire to wear an 'invisibility cloak'.

In this chapter I want to explore all the ways that we can continue to engage with the world of fashion on our own terms in order to cultivate a confident and stylish image. I need to say, loudly and clearly, that these ideas are not intended to dictate what you should wear. The aim is to help you to make better and more considered choices when you are shopping for clothes. I have come to the conclusion that the best approach is to become less concerned about the latest fashion and more focused on creating a 'look' which reflects our personality, lifestyle, self-image, size and shape. That way we can avoid all the pitfalls of looking (dreaded words) 'matronly' or 'dowdy'. There has to be a nod to fashion in order to achieve this, however, because every season there are subtle changes in cut and shape, which means that sticking with the same old, same old can lead you into a cul-de-sac firmly stuck in a huge rut!

The
HOPE
FASHION
STORY
by Nayna
McIntosh

WHEN I TURNED FIFTY, I realised that I was more than halfway through my life! I had a very successful corporate career with M&S at the time and before that had been a key member of the team that launched the George clothing brand in 1989 and then Per Una in 2001, both of which were groundbreaking concepts in their time. Yet as I looked around the high street, there was little on offer that was sensitive to how a woman of my age might want to dress or shop.

NAYNA (SECOND LEFT)
AND THE LFF TEAM

So I decided to follow my instincts, give up my corporate job and offer something genuinely different that would help to give some confidence back to women of a certain age. I founded Hope in September 2015 with a clear ambition to establish a fashion brand that would embrace women of all shapes and sizes, and in particular women from their forties onwards.

When I shared my idea with a group of close friends and colleagues their response and excitement gave me huge encouragement to take the next step. Soon I had assembled a team of designers and product specialists with over 200 years' experience, an average age of fifty-two, and five out of six of them were women. Together we developed a unique approach to sizing which focused on body shape rather than numbers – do you know anyone who wants to be called 'extra-large'?! We also created the Hope Code, a guide to styling that helps women to accentuate what they love about themselves and draw attention away from what they're less confident about.

Hope's authenticity has helped to create an emotional connection between the brand and its customers. I have been taken aback by the response – so many customers have said that they had given up hope of ever finding anything that would make them feel comfortable, stylish or sexy ever again. I feel immensely proud to have helped so many women feel good about themselves for the first time in ages.

Style v Fashion – What is the difference?

/ **Style is personal. Fashion is universal.** Ageing can render us lost and directionless in the world of fashion, which has no desire to engage with our needs. Being stylish is about choosing clothes and accessories that say something about who you are. It's about knowing yourself and what suits your shape. It's also about how you see yourself and how you want the world to see you.

/ **Style is ageless. Fashion is ageist.** The latest fashions are rarely showcased on older models for a good reason – they may or may not work on an older body while they will invariably work on the very young, tall, thin models on whom they are invariably shown. Fashion is associated with the avant-garde, the new and the trendy. These ideas are the very antithesis of what I want from clothes right now. I don't crave novelty and reinvention; I just crave something that reflects who I am. Fashion is continually travelling towards youth, which is why it has little to say to women who are going in the opposite direction. I don't want to emulate the style of a teenager, nor do I want to look old-fashioned.

> **If you develop a strong, enduring style you don't have to keep changing your wardrobe every season.**

/ Style is enduring. Fashion is fleeting. If you develop a strong, enduring style you don't have to keep changing your wardrobe every season. You can update your clothes by selecting what works best for you from the current trends. The key word here is 'update'. Unfortunately, it doesn't mean just buying the same things you have always bought from the same shops. I have a penchant for black trousers but the cut and shape of these quite utilitarian items change constantly, so I do try to keep up with what is currently in vogue.

/ Style is knowing your best colours. Fashion is about 'this season's colour'. I have read three articles this week saying that yellow is the 'must-have' colour this season. But yellow looks terrible on people with cool skin tones like me and doesn't always suit people with warm tones either. I dislike the way that the dictates of fashion assume that these trends will suit everyone – clearly they cannot and don't – regardless of age.

/ Style is what suits you. Fashion is what suits the designer's vision. Women come in many shapes and sizes. Fashion models don't. If you are short and wide you may struggle to find great clothes but (as I will show you) it is perfectly possible to dress with flair and panache. It's a question of understanding proportions and then working with your physique, rather than fighting the facts of your figure. When I finally worked out how to draw attention to my 'best bits', which are all above the waist, I not only felt more comfortable, I felt more like the best version of 'me'.

/ Style can incorporate comfort. Fashion has no interest in being comfortable. Comfortable clothes have become much more interesting to me as I have aged. When I say comfort I am not talking about elasticated waists, although they too have their place as long as it's not on a pair of beige Crimplene trousers from the Classics range in Marks

& Spencer! I am talking about comfortable fabrics like cashmere jumpers from Uniqlo or velvet opaque tights from Wolford. I am also talking about cut. I need to have sleeves in blouses or dresses that allow me to lift my arms above my head (to fix my hair and makeup), not cut off all circulation above the elbow.

/ Style is easier when you are older. Fashion is easier when you are younger. Think of the most stylish woman you know – is she really young or a bit older? It seems to me that you need to have lived for a while before you can develop a distinctive personal style unless you are in the fashion industry. I think that this is where we older women can really make our mark. Ironically, it was our generation of women, who came of age in the Sixties, who created our current problems. In the Fifties, girls longed for the moment when they would start to look like younger versions of their own mothers. We were all so avid for the distinctive youth-oriented fashion typified by Twiggy's miniskirts and baby-doll dresses that we seem to have destroyed the possibility of a distinctive 'grown-up' style for fear of being seen as matronly or a total frump.

/

When I finally worked out how to draw attention to my 'best bits', which are all above the waist, I not only felt more comfortable, I felt more like the best version of 'me'.

Style Tribes and the Older Woman

A while ago I came across a wickedly funny article by Virginia Ironside in the *Sunday Times* called: *'Don't Let It Go: Too Many Women Give Up On Their Looks As They Age'*. At the start of the article, Ironside quotes Eleanor Roosevelt: 'Beautiful young people are accidents of nature, but beautiful old people are works of art.'

> **If you would like to develop a stronger sense of style, a good starting point is to decide which style tribe you might belong to.**

Of course there are older women like Iris Apfel and Sue Kreitzman who take this quite literally by turning themselves into colourful *objets d'art*, but I understand the quote to mean that being seen as beautiful as we age takes thought and effort, while for the young it can be effortless. Ironside starts by berating what she calls the 'service station look', which she describes thus: 'They [older women] drag on some trackie bottoms, bung on a beige top, get their grey hair cut by the man round the corner, and adopt what I call the service station look – service stations being places where these asexual, betrousered, make-up-less . . . old lumps seem to congregate.'

I am assuming that the very fact you are reading this book implies that you are very aware of the pitfalls of the service station look. I see it everywhere and it makes me feel quite sad and a bit desperate. Mainly because it is an act of surrender to invisibility, irrelevancy and the self-effacement that some believe must come with age.

If you would like to develop a stronger sense of style, a good starting point is to decide which style tribe you might belong to. It's easy to mock some of these, as Ironside does, but they are useful as a way to think about what each tribe can teach us, both good and bad. For each, I have tried to come up with an example of a woman who really encapsulates this style in the most interesting way.

Tribe One

/

THE ANTI-FASHION LOOK

This is about old money and an old-school approach. Clothes are of enduring quality, conservative in style, and kept and worn for years. Colours and shapes are classic, shoes are sensible and comfortable, and jewellery is discreet and inherited. This is an unshowy, traditional and quality-led style which can easily look staid and frumpy. The Queen is probably the best example of how to make this look work beautifully, both on and off duty. She regularly appears on 'best dressed' lists and for good reason. Her Majesty is neither tall nor thin but her beautifully cut clothes in a single block of colour work perfectly on her mature body.

Good lesson to learn: Always buy the very best quality you can afford.

THE QUEEN/ TRIBE ONE

ANNA WINTOUR/ TRIBE THREE

ZANDRA RHODES/ TRIBE TWO

Tribe Two

/

THE FUN LOOK

This is typified by the Jenny Joseph poem which starts: *'When I am an old woman I shall wear purple / With a red hat which doesn't go, and doesn't suit me.'* It seems to be informed by an attitude of 'who are you to say what's appropriate?' So this look encompasses mad hair colours, zany prints and any other eccentricities to signal non-conformity and a devil-may-care approach. Zandra Rhodes pulls off the Fun Look rather brilliantly, but as a renowned dress designer she's always had pink hair and brightly coloured clothes in her own distinctive fabrics. Another good exponent of this style is Sarah Jane Adams (aka Saramai) who also has a strong and highly coloured quirky personal style.

Good lesson to learn: Don't be afraid of bright or clashing colours.

Tribe Three

/

THE HIGH-FASHION LOOK

Older women who can afford designer clothes are probably responsible for keeping the fashion industry alive. This look is all about conspicuous consumption of expensive labels with logos on evident display. The well-toned arm will sport the latest 'it' bag, and jewellery will be expensive and from smart jewellers. This look has high-maintenance hair in a stylish cut and colour, a high-maintenance body and seeks 'agelessness'. In real life, Anna Wintour probably pulls it off best. As the editor of American *Vogue*, Wintour is seen on every front row wearing designer clothes and always has an immaculate self-presentation.

Good lesson to learn: Grooming is never out of fashion.

Tribe Four

/

THE BOHEMIAN LOOK

This is all about comfortable dressing in a creative and arty way. Clothes will be flowing, loose, and may also have bright and colourful elements such as yellow tights and a yellow scarf. Sometimes unstructured and messy, the hair may be grey or dyed into a deep hennaed orange or plummy shade. Jewellery will be large, chunky and ethnic, and may be in unusual materials. Esme Young, the distinctive judge on *The Great British Sewing Bee*, is an example of how original this look can be. Esme's grey hair has been cut into a sharp, precise, fringed bob and she also chooses distinctive eyewear.

Good lesson to learn: Surprising eye-catching jewellery and glasses can transform an outfit.

Tribe Five

/

THE ENGLISH COUNTRYWOMAN LOOK

A life filled with dog walking and/or horse riding, so clothes have to be practical and no-nonsense. A wax jacket, jeans tucked into green Hunter wellies to cope with the mud, or low-heeled shoes. Colours are muted, fabrics durable and jewellery is traditional (pearls are a favourite). Hair is kept to the same style, often for life. For dressier occasions the favourite black dress is pulled from the recesses of the wardrobe and enlivened with a bright scarf over one shoulder or an amusing ethnic-inspired jacket. Jilly Cooper and Camilla, Duchess of Cornwall come to mind.

Good lesson to learn: Comfort and practicality matter too.

Tribe Six

/

THE ROCK CHICK LOOK

This is the rebellious older woman who wants to kick over the traces
and show that she is still young at heart. She gets her first tattoo at
sixty as a shock tactic and wears leather, studs, decorated high boots
(maybe above the knee), mostly in black. Her hair may be dyed back
to its original colour or have a brightly coloured strip to signal the fight
against convention. Jewellery will be mostly silver and worn as rings,
earrings or bracelets. Debbie Harry (Blondie) rocks this look very
successfully.

Good lesson to learn: Reinvention is possible as we age.

Tribe Seven

/

THE BUSINESSWOMAN
OR TOP POLITICIAN LOOK

This used to be about 'power dressing' and I can well remember my
shoulder-padded masculine trouser suits of the 1980s! Nowadays,
women tend to wear slightly softer shapes, dresses (often with a
matching jacket) and small heels to signal femininity, and dark colours
to signal authority. Jackets are still important for more formal occasions,
especially in a male-dominated setting, but clothes need to say 'I mean
business' without appearing masculine. Hair is neat and no-nonsense.
Discrete jewellery, belts and low-heeled shoes may be used to add an
interesting and surprising element. Theresa May and Nicola Sturgeon
have this down to a fine art by looking confident and businesslike.

Good lesson to learn: Clothes can be used to signal confidence.

Tribe Eight

/

SERIOUSLY COOL STYLE

This is exemplified by women like Linda Rodin and 'Accidental Icon' Lyn Slater. These two very slim, beautiful American women have white hair and are effortlessly chic. Slater is invariably photographed wearing black-and-white clothes and favours avant-garde Japanese designers. She always sports big black-and-white earrings and sunglasses. Rodin favours denim and is usually photographed in her very cool apartment with her very cool dog.

Good lesson to learn: A modern hairstyle makes all the difference.

Tribe Nine

/

CHIC FRENCH STYLE

For the older stylish French woman, clothes are about creating a wonderfully understated yet sexually alluring look without appearing to have made any effort whatsoever. Her plain jumper will always be cashmere and the scarf artlessly tied at the neck will be silk and probably by Hermès. Her underwear will be as beautiful as the top layer and will be matching. Her hair will be well cut, immaculate and shiny, and her real jewellery will be discreet rather than blingy. She likes blocks of strong colour and eschews patterns. Shoes invariably have a high heel to show off her excellent legs in sheer stockings. Inès de La Fressange and Christine Lagarde show how it's done.

Good lesson to learn: Classic and chic definitely doesn't have to be boring – and underwear matters too.

INES DE LA FRESSANGE/ TRIBE NINE

Choosing an Individual Style

There is much to learn from the style tribes, both the pitfalls and the good things they can teach us. I naturally gravitate towards a simple, pared-down classic look which is closest to the businesswoman style, but in my heart I aspire to the chic French look, while lacking that elusive *je ne sais quoi*, probably because I was born on the wrong side of the Channel! The problem with my style is that I often choose very safe, quite boring clothes in a limited palette of black, navy and grey. However, I have definitely learned something from the fun and bohemian styles and now inject more colour with some bolder scarves and pieces of statement jewellery, especially earrings and sunglasses. I also think I could take a leaf out of the anti-fashion style book by buying fewer, better-quality clothes.

> **I aspire to the chic French look, while lacking that elusive *je ne sais quoi*, probably because I was born on the wrong side of the Channel!**

The following section is designed to help you to make better choices so that you can find a style that reflects your personality and lifestyle and helps you to steer well clear of the dreaded 'service station look'. It will give you useful information about shapes, colours and accessories which you might find work better for your body. They are ideas, suggestions and pointers for those of you who would like some help and guidance to make informed decisions when searching for that needle in a haystack: a wearable wardrobe!

Body Shape

Let's start with the basic proportions of your body. Think about whether you are bigger at the bust, the waist or the hips, or maybe your bust and hips are the same and the waist smaller, or your bust, waist and hips are a similar size. Alternatively, you may be petite or short and plump.

Each of these shapes has particular needs which will indicate what you need to think about when you are looking for clothes to suit you.

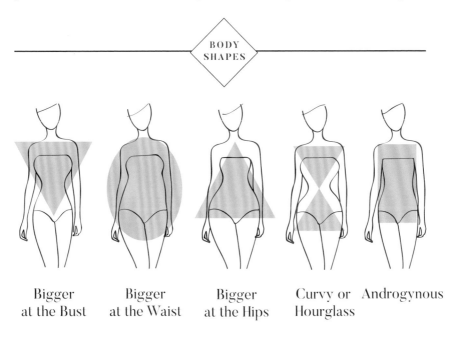

BODY SHAPES

| Bigger at the Bust | Bigger at the Waist | Bigger at the Hips | Curvy or Hourglass | Androgynous |

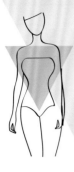

BIGGER AT THE BUST

Your bust is larger than both your waist and hips as an inverted triangle. The most important consideration here is to elongate the body and balance the generous bosom with the much slimmer bottom half of your body. You can achieve this a number of ways:

1/ Choose an A-line rather than a straight skirt which would accentuate your slim lower half.

2/ Use some subtle padding on the shoulders. This sounds counterintuitive but it will help the rounded top area to look more balanced.

3/ Don't cut yourself in half at the waist with a belt or change of colour. Go for a single colour from neck to hem.

4/ Wear V-necklines and wrap-style tops to 'split' the bust. Round or boat necks can make the bosom look like a shelf. Use long pendants or necklaces that also break up the expanse of the bust area.

5/ If you have lovely slim legs draw attention to them with your tights and shoes.

6/ Trousers can have pockets and pleats to add width to very narrow hips to create balance.

7/ Keep sleeves slim and narrow and choose hats which have a small brim. Alternatively, wear a tall fascinator to add height.

BIGGER AT THE WAIST
– THE OVAL SHAPE

The waist is either bigger or a similar size to the hips. This might be a shape you have acquired after the menopause and no amount of diet or exercise seems to affect it.

1/ The top of the oval may include rounded shoulders, so lightly pad with shoulder pads to improve the shape of tops and dresses.

2/ Don't wear oversized and baggy clothes as these will make you look bigger. Wear clothes that skim the body but which are not tight.

3/ Draw attention away from your middle. A great haircut, beautiful makeup and a bright scarf or bold necklace draw attention upwards, and colourful tights or shoes can draw attention downwards if you have great legs.

4/ Keep colours simple and clothes classic rather than quirky.

BIGGER AT
THE HIPS

The classic pear shape, of which I am an excellent example, having always had 'heavy' legs – biggish thighs, calves and ankles. I also have a much smaller waist-to-hip measurement and smaller breasts.

1/ Keep all the interest on and above the waist. Colour and pattern are best kept to this area. Light colours enlarge, while dark colours reduce, so clothe the bottom half in the darkest shades.

2/ Go to town on hair, makeup and earrings to keep attention on the top half. Scarves can also be bright and colourful and add interest.

3/ Structured padded shoulders are a good way to make them slightly wider to balance the hips.

4/ Choose very smooth narrow or straight-legged trousers with a narrow waistband. Looser shapes can work too if you are tall enough.

5/ If you wear a skirt or dress, choose matching tights and shoes to elongate the legs. Tuck narrow trousers into high boots in the same colour.

CURVY OR HOURGLASS

Bust and hips are a similar size and you have a smaller waist, so you can either go for a sexy look or something more toned down if you want to have authority in a business context.

1/ You usually have great legs so you can wear sheer tights and you will probably look better with a heel, however small.

2/ If you want to draw attention to your waist, wear a belt to cinch it and divide the top from the bottom half.

3/ Wear a pencil skirt which narrows at the bottom or a belted dress with a straight skirt.

4/ You will look feminine in a masculine suit so go for sharply tailored trouser suits worn with a softer blouse.

5/ Beware of deeply plunging necklines unless you still have a great décolletage and want to draw attention to the fact!

ANDROGYNOUS

Bust, waist and hips are a similar size
so you are an oblong shape.

1/ Have a change of colour at the
waist and hemline to create
stop points for the eye so that
you look less straight up and
down.

2/ Wear shorter, rounder
necklaces rather than long
beads or pendants.

3/ If you are long in the body,
wear high-waisted trousers
with a wider waistband to
make legs look longer.

4/ Use horizontal stripes to
add width and avoid a single
colour from top to toe.

5/ A belt is a great way to
create the illusion of a waist,
especially if you have a fuller
blouse tucked in.

SLIM PETITES

You are shorter than 5'3" and a size 6 to 8. You may have always been tiny thanks to an efficient metabolism (lucky you).

1/ Separates are easier to buy than dresses as the waist can be too low.

2/ Wearing different colours on the top and bottom half may make you look shorter.

3/ Have sleeves shortened if necessary. Too-long sleeves will make you look shorter and the dress, coat, jacket or blouse too big.

4/ Stick to simple shapes that fit you well in sophisticated colours so that you don't look too 'doll-like'.

5/ You can do quirky well, so look for unusual accessories and scarves.

NON-SLIM PETITES

This is possibly the hardest body shape to find clothes to fit as larger sizes also tend to assume you are taller.

1/ If you wear separates keep the colours similar and darker.

2/ Top-to-toe block colours look best for dresses, with a piece of bold statement jewellery at the neck.

3/ Keep shapes simple and classy. No frills or fussiness.

4/ Choose ankle boots which finish at the narrowest point of the ankle rather than knee-high boots.

5/ Make statements with your hair, makeup, jewellery.

BARBARA
petite

A Fabulous Fit

A while ago I was bemoaning the fact that I had just bought a pair of trousers and was dissatisfied with the fit. I had tried on both the smaller and larger sizes which were no good, so had bought the least worse option. The friend I was talking to said, 'Why not get them altered to fit you?' This simply hadn't occurred to me but I really think that this might be the solution whenever I stand in a changing room and love the outfit but dislike some aspect of how it fits me. Maybe only appropriate for a special occasion, but well worth considering.

How to Choose the Most Flattering Colour Palette

The final element to creating a fabulous style is knowing which colours suit you. I need to start by clarifying that this is about looking your absolute best. If you are cool-toned and you love mustard, then wear mustard. I say this as someone who once bought a mustard sweater because it was that season's must-have colour. I never actually wore this desired object and kept taking it off because I knew it didn't do me any favours but couldn't pinpoint why. When I subsequently 'had my colours done', it was very clear that, as a cool-toned 'winter', this was the last colour I should have gone for.

I know that this subject creates great doubts and confusion, so I will try to make it as straightforward as possible. In the chapter on makeup I have explained that our skin undertone tends to be either yellow or blue, although confusingly it can sometimes be neutral. Remember that this is not so much about hair and eye colour but skin tone and it doesn't change when your hair goes grey.

TOP TIPS

for IMPROVING THE FIT OF YOUR CLOTHES

01 Choose trousers in stretchier fabrics that will fit better and bag less around the bottom. I find this certainly works better for me.

02 Bust darts may not fit in the right place if the bosom is lower-slung. This may be easily solved if you wear a really good, well-fitting bra and tighten the straps.

03 Most shoulders can be improved with subtle shoulder pads. We are not talking about the monstrosities routinely sewn into clothes in the Eighties! These smaller versions are a useful corrective to poor posture.

04 Knees are never a very attractive feature, whether young or old, fat or thin. Legs look better when hem lengths hit just below the knee, where the leg is narrowest.

This is preferable to a hem that sits at the chunkiest part of the calf.

05 Sleeves are a godsend to we older women. I wish there were shops that only sold sleeved dresses and tops. Elbows are rarely pretty, so go for a bracelet length which hits at the narrowest part of the wrist and can show off nice jewellery.

06 Very high necklines are really hard for me to wear now. I like the look of them but they accentuate my jowls! Boat necks work well if you don't want to expose the skin and can look prettier than round necks. V-neck shapes work best with a bigger *embonpoint*.

SUE

COOL BLUE UNDERTONES

You may have had your colours done and you have been told that you are 'winter' or 'summer'. Winters will suit the darkest tones of their best colours and summers will look better in the paler shades of the following colour palette. You may have naturally black, platinum or brown hair with no red tones and blue or grey eyes.

<u>You will look better in:</u>
- **Reds:** cherry and plummy shades, all shades of pink from palest to most vibrant, but avoid scarlet and orangey-reds.
- **Blues:** ice-cold pale blue, air-force blue and navy.
- **Greens:** jade and pale fern green; avoid citric lime greens.
- **White, grey, black** and **purple** are all good choices.
- You probably suit **silver** rather than gold jewellery.

JULIA

WARM YELLOW UNDERTONES

You have been told that you are 'autumn' or 'spring'. You may be a redhead or have natural reddish tones in your hair and brown eyes. But be careful – you may have had reddish tones added as high- or lowlights and these will only work well if you are definitely warm-toned.

<u>You will look better in:</u>
- **Reds:** scarlet, rusts, orangey-reds, corals work best.
- **Blues:** these are harder to get right but go for greeny-blues.
- **Yellows** and **browns:** all yellow, brown, mustard-toned shades will work as long as they are not pale lemon.
- **Greens:** avoid blue-toned greens and embrace clear sharp greens and lime.
- **Avoid pure white, grey** and **black** which might make you look drained. **Cream, navy** and **purple** all work well with warm-toned skins.

Another place to find clothes is in sales, fashion outlets and charity shops. This is more of a lottery in terms of size availability and the quality of the goods on offer, but with a good eye and a sensible approach bargains can be had. My friend Penny Kocher (aka the Frugal Fashion Shopper) gave me her top tips so that you can avoid all the poor-quality clothes that may be found in charity shops:

1 /
Research the area and surrounding areas where you live and decide which shop has the best stock.

2 /
Learn which shops have the most reasonable pricing policy. Things should be £7, not £70.

3 /
Never drop your standards. You are not there to buy rubbish but recognisable labels and brands.

4 /
Try not to impulse buy. Buy to fill a gap in your wardrobe, not to fill up your wardrobe.

5 /
Have fun and experiment, which you can do with a skirt costing £3, so that if the experiment is a mistake it's not a costly one.

6 /
You can get an adrenaline rush when you find something original and you are recycling clothes!

THE BESPOKE ROUTE

There is another route for occasion dressing if you have very deep pockets and that is to go to a couturier and have a dress, suit or coat and dress made from scratch in a colour and material of your choice. I have done this only once when I decided to treat myself to a really special cocktail dress for my sixtieth birthday party. I really enjoyed the process, which involves an initial consultation, the creation of a toile for fitting purposes, then the choosing of fabric, followed by several visits as the garment progresses towards completed perfection. If you can afford it or just want to push the boat out for a very special occasion, having something bespoke, designed and made just for you, is the very best way to end up with the perfect outfit for your size, shape and personality.

As I get older I am enjoying clothes as much, if not more than, I have ever done. I am determined to look as interesting and stylish as possible and to confront the ageism of the fashion industry by engaging with it on my own terms. But how I wish that shops were interested in stocking the kind of clothes that I want to wear and which work better on my ageing body, but I suspect that is unlikely to happen anytime soon. In the meantime, I will keep looking and experimenting by trying things on and rooting out the odd gem to add some interest to my wardrobe. Fabulous style isn't a wardrobe full of designer labels – it's a great pair of earrings, a beautiful scarf, a single flash of colour or anything else that you choose in order to say: 'Look at me, I am a confident, stylish and fabulous older woman and I refuse to be invisible.'

Fabulous
Hair

Beautiful hair has long been synonymous with youthful vigour, health and sexual allure.

There is a reason it's called our 'crowning glory': because we wear it daily atop our heads as a symbol of our femininity. However, like makeup and fashion, hair style is not straightforward as we age because there are societal pressures around both colour and length. I actually had no idea what a contentious subject hair is for older women before I posted what I thought was a stunning photograph of Nicola Griffin onto our Facebook page. Nicky was doing her very first photo shoot for specialist haircare company White Hot Hair and Look Fabulous Forever was doing the makeup for the session. The photo showed her stunning long, thick, lustrous grey locks in all their glory and I expected hundreds of 'likes' and 'shares'. What I didn't anticipate were comments like 'I hate long grey hair on older women' and 'she looks ridiculous at her age with that hairstyle'. I was amazed at the vehemence with which Nicky was criticised for having her particular combination of hair colour and length.

I am therefore addressing the subject of fabulous hair for all us older women with some trepidation, but, as before, these are ideas rather than rules and, as with makeup and clothes, we have earned the right to style our hair in whatever way we choose. However, there are some considerations to take on board, such as what might suit your face, and also better practices when it comes to haircare which I want to explore. I've already suggested that the best way to look and feel better about yourself is to apply some lovely makeup and learn which clothes styles suit you. I'd also suggest that the third is to get a really good haircut. My routine every day is: choose something nice to wear, put my face on, and finally fix my hair. I have chosen a very low-maintenance short style for my poker-straight hair. I get it cut when it feels straggly

or just 'won't go' and usually have some bright silvery white highlights added at the front. My hair is very slowly going grey and I just wish it would hurry up! In the meantime, my hairdresser adds some strands of brighter colour round my face. I then wash and blow-dry it myself every few days. In the morning I brush it through, create some height at the crown with a bit of backcombing (I know what you're thinking but it's the only way to create some volume on top) and then I apply a light spray to hold it. I rarely touch my hair again until bedtime, which means I can ignore it and get on with my busy life. I would love to have longer, messier, more carefree-looking hair, which is currently fashionable. However, that apparently effortless look is deceptively high-maintenance, and I just don't have that kind of hair or life.

How to Wash Your Hair: My Top Tips

◆ Surfactants in the shampoo cleanse both the scalp and the hair and conditioners supply positively charged surfactants which sit on the hair to make it smoother and easier to untangle.

◆ Wash your hair by working a small amount of shampoo into the scalp and massaging it gently into the roots, then work down to the rest of the hair, trying not to create knots. Rinse for twice as long as the time it took to wash it.

◆ If you are using a conditioner after shampooing, just add it to the ends rather than the roots and then use a wide-toothed comb to disperse it evenly. Then give the hair a final rinse.

◆ Squeeze out excess water and then pat rather than rub dry with a towel to lessen damage from the friction generated, and again comb through gently with a wide-toothed comb.

TOP TIPS

for BLOW-DRYING YOUR HAIR

01 First I apply a **styling gel**. Currently I am using something by Kérastase called Lift Vertige, mainly because I love the idea of a vertiginous lift!

02 I have **three types of brush with bristles** that are all circular and of different diameters to suit the differing lengths of my haircut: large, medium and small. The purpose of the brushes is to create volume and height, rather than curl. My hair won't curl however hard I try, so I don't try.

03 I work round my head in **sections** with the appropriate-sized brush by lifting the hair and then using the hairdryer to dry each strand as it is wound around the brush. I also spray some extra-volumising spray into the roots at that point to get extra lift, which is rarely vertiginous!

04 When my hair is thoroughly dry, I often use a '**hot brush**' to smooth any clumpy frizzy ends. This is a large round brush which, like a hairdryer, has warm air blowing through it which helps to style the hair very easily. I then finish with a bit of subtle backcombing on top (I hate flat hair on me) and a quick spritz of hairspray.

05 If my hair looks very flat and needs a bit of oomph, I use White Hot Hair's Shooshing Crème which I rub into my palms and lightly coat the top and front so that it's more manageable.

Hairdressing Then and Now

Thinking back, I suspect that one of the reasons our mothers and grandmothers looked old before their time was down to the way they had their hair done. Remember the 'blue-rinse brigade' and the way that grey hair was routinely tortured into neat sausages of curls in a weekly shampoo and set? This involved my mother going to the hairdresser and having her hair cut into uniform short layers. Rollers were then put in over the whole head and the 'victim' (sorry, customer) was shoved under a massive metal dome to have hot air blasted onto her head for about half an hour. I think this timing was more to do with fitting as many victims as possible into the appointment schedule than any need to be cooked for so long. After this torture, made considerably worse by menopausal hot flushes, the hair was brushed through, teased into shape with a bit of backcombing and then set with hairspray to create a nice rigid effect which, as long as you wore a hairnet at night, would last until the next appointment. Every two or three months, my mum would undergo even more torture when harsh and very smelly chemicals would be squeezed onto the hair, which was twisted round special tiny rollers to create the much-desired 'permanent wave'.

No wonder that in the Sixties we were desperate for an alternative! In 1966 I was chosen to be the carnival queen for my local town in Suffolk. The prize included a perm and a month's worth of shampoo and sets at the local hair salon run by an old man called Mr Ward. I adamantly refused to take up the prize and insisted that my mother avail herself of the benefit in my place. Fortunately, she was more than happy to do so. I was eighteen at the time and was already in thrall to Mary Quant's wonderful straight, glossy, geometric precision cut by Vidal Sassoon and Sandy Shaw's longer version with a full fringe and loose swinging curtains of shiny hair either side of her face. The shampoo and set were out, and sharp, precise-cutting was in, followed

by blow-drying with a hand-held hairdryer and a round brush to 'dress' the hair. Sometimes hair was piled on top of the head in elaborately curled styles (remember Dusty Springfield?), which required hair pieces and tons of hairspray, but most of us wanted our hair to look sleek, shiny and modern.

Hairdressing today is not so different from how it was after the revolution in cutting techniques started by Vidal Sassoon. There may still exist salons that cater for the permed, shampoo-and-set, old lady look, but they must be on their last legs. Nowadays, hairdressers have to perform miracles with their scissors and colourants because we all want our hair to look as near as possible to how it was when we were younger – thick, glossy and luxuriant – and it seems that we will go to endless trouble to achieve such a result, probably because hair is so emblematic of youthful vigour and attractiveness.

Hair Colour and Age

I love the French expression *éminence grise*. It means a person who exercises power or influence in a certain sphere without holding an official position – a bit like a lot of women! Translated, it would be a 'grey eminence', which implies that this power behind the throne is older – hence their grey hair. I heartily wish that grey hair was seen as a similar badge of honour, indicating strength, wisdom and experience, rather than an embarrassing and shameful sign of ageing. I am very perverse when it comes to hair colour and ageing. I actually prefer to see older women with naturally grey or white hair and have longed for mine to go properly grey for the past ten years. I have known for a long time that my cool-toned skin would really suit grey hair, so I have been convincing my various hairdressers for years to give me proper silver highlights instead of what they thought I should have wanted, which was light blonde streaks. As my hair slowly turns grey I am loving it more and more, and I often hold a mirror so that I can see the crown where it's a lovely natural silver colour. I get so excited by the prospect of it being that colour all over my head.

I think part of the reason that many women feel very differently from me is because the first grey hairs can appear as early as our thirties. This happens as we begin to lose melanin, the pigmentation in our cells which is responsible for our natural hair colour. This very visible sign of ageing, which we have learned to associate with something dreadful, may cause real distress over the next twenty years as the melanin loss gathers pace, so that by our fifties it is quite usual for 50 per cent of our hair to be grey. The speed with which this happens can be affected by hormones, nutrition, stress and general health, but it's mostly down to genetic inheritance – if your mother or father was prematurely grey then there's a high chance that you will be too.

GETTING THE *BEST* FROM YOUR HAIRDRESSER

Here's how to work with your hairdresser so that you get exactly what you want:

1/ Ask how you can look your best given your hair colour, texture and face shape.

2/ Tell them every problem you have with your hair – kink, dryness, styling, etc. – as there are new techniques and products being developed all the time. For instance, if you wake up with matted hair there is a new product called 'pillow proof hair'. Who knew?

3/ Think about seasonal changes and adjustments you might need to make to your hairstyle. For instance, if you wear scarves in the winter you may need it shorter at the back so that it still sits well with a high collar and scarf.

4/ Say how much time you have to spend on your hair at home and how adept you are at styling it yourself.

5/ Discuss appropriate tools, including brushes and nozzles on your hairdryer. Ask about being taught how to blow-dry your hair properly if you are unsure. For instance, using clips and sectioning the hair and using mirrors to see the back will all help to improve the finish.

6/ If you are getting a new hairstyle or colour, discuss what needs to change in your home haircare routine.

Fabulous Grey Hair

Grey hair may have lost melanin but it doesn't have to look dull, dry and lifeless. Hair consists of around 150,000 individual strands, emerging from our hair follicles at the rate of around a centimetre a month. The hair that we see as our crowning glory is actually dead protein (keratin), as are our finger- and toenails, but it is nevertheless a very visible barometer of our health. The body doesn't recognise hair as essential tissue, so if we are ill, or there is a deficit of proteins, carbohydrates, vitamins or minerals, our hair will be the first to suffer. Lifestyle can also contribute to this deficit and, as you would expect, it's all the usual suspects. Smoking, excess alcohol and lack of sleep will not only make your skin look grey, but will make your hair look less than lustrous.

> **Hair consists of around 150,000 individual strands, emerging from our hair follicles at the rate of around a centimetre a month.**

Therefore, any improvements we make to our general wellbeing will be a bonus for our hair. Primarily, we need to eat a diet that supplies all the necessary nutrients, including enough good sources of first-class protein. Meat, oily fish and eggs consist of essential amino acids which are both abundant and easily absorbed. Deficiencies of iron, calcium, vitamins D, B12 and B6 may affect hair health, so eat foods that supply these or, if you are a vegetarian, you may need to take them in the form of a supplement.

TOP TIPS

for A HEALTHY HEAD OF HAIR

01 General health affects hair health first so a diet rich in beneficial nutrients will pay dividends and result in a head of glossier, thicker hair (see pages 202–9).

02 Scalp health is important too. Improve with massage to increase blood flow to the hair follicles. Surfactants in shampoo clean away any dirt, pollution, sebum and skin cells.

03 If you decide to completely cover grey hair with a permanent hair dye, best to go to a qualified colourist as it will involve strong chemicals. A good hairdresser will ensure that this is done safely and in a way that maintains healthy hair.

04 Wet hair is especially vulnerable. Conditioners help to smooth the hair after washing so that you can untangle it with a wide-toothed comb. Don't brush, yank or pull the hair.

05 Remember that excessive heat from styling tools may cause permanent damage to the hair shaft. Always use the lower heat settings on hairdryers.

KATE

Transitioning to Grey

I think this process is what keeps a lot of older women dyeing their hair. They just don't know how to go about it. Also, their hairdresser might be less than helpful given that most salons depend on expensive colour treatments to make a profit. I am transitioning myself at the moment. About ten years ago I decided to have silver/ashy highlights added to my brown hair. Over time this created a solid colour of grey/ash-blonde hair with a naturally dark bit around the bottom at the back of my head. I was still getting regrowth of darker roots, especially around my hairline, so every two months or so I'd go to the hairdresser for a half-head of highlights to keep the whole effect nice and bright. I realised that this regrowth was becoming less of an issue, so I decided to have fewer and fewer silvery-white highlights added. Now I just have a few strands of colour at the very front, which is less time-consuming and less costly, and the rest of my hair is now almost completely grey. Eventually, I will stop adding the highlights at the front and see how it looks and hopefully I will be done with colouring my hair forever!

JOSEPHINE'S
STORY

How I transitioned to grey . . .

My hair was naturally very dark brown and the first grey hairs appeared in my late twenties, so I started to dye it and continued to do so for about twenty years. I knew it was affecting the condition of my hair and that dark brown/ black was beginning to look 'hard' and unnatural. We were living in South Africa, it was summertime; it was hot and humid. I was tired of colouring then pinning it up. I hadn't planned it – I decided to stop colouring it on impulse! I was in my early fifties and just felt I was ready to accept the next season in my life. The process of going from dark to light was drastic!! I went from long, dark to cropped overnight. My hairdresser cut it initially, but not short enough so I had a friend finish it off. It then took another couple of cuts to get rid of the dark tips. I hadn't told anyone I was going to do it and initially my daughter, who was still at primary school, was shocked but it wasn't long before she accepted it, and my husband loved it. And fortunately all but one of my friends loved it too.

I am in my sixties now and I absolutely love my white/grey hair and would never change it. To any women thinking of doing what I did ten years ago, I would say, 'Go for it!' Not everyone has to do it as drastically as I did, but funnily enough, my mother had done exactly the same thing at a similar age, so maybe I was just following her example.

TOP TIPS

for TRANSITIONING TO GREY

01 Switch to a shade in a semi-permanent colour if you have been colouring all over with permanent colour. If you have been going much darker, switch to a slightly lighter shade that will blend better with your roots.

02 You will be ready for a haircut and a colour touch-up in six weeks. Remove as much length as you are comfortable with. It's best to get rid of all your coloured hair as swiftly as possible so you can start afresh. Repeat your same colour as last time or a lighter one, continuing with your slightly more grey-embracing shade and technique.

03 In six more weeks, get another cut but leave your roots alone this time. This might be the hardest part – so grit your teeth and keep going!

04 Keep getting your hair trimmed every six weeks and, if you really hate the 'two-toned' colour, have a few highlights added with a semi-permanent colour to blend the natural colour and the remains of the dyed hair.

05 Two more haircuts and you should be able to continue growing and cutting your hair at your own rate. You've done it! Now you can fully embrace the grey without having to worry about colour any more.

THE WHITE HOT STORY
BEGAN IN 2011 when, after
a lifetime of dyeing my hair, my
inspired hairdresser suggested
I stop dyeing and discover what
was underneath. Going from 'faux
brown' to white opened my eyes to
the 'beauty taboo' of revealing your
grey hair, and I was determined
to do something to change the
perception that ditching the dye
means 'letting yourself go'. At the
same time, I soon learned that
white hair is porous, often unruly
and needs special care if it is to
look its best, and when I couldn't
find a great regime that performed
well and felt upbeat and positive,
I decided to create my own. I
launched White Hot in 2013 and
women all over the world are now
sharing their positive experiences
about loving their white and grey
hair and proving that embracing
the grey is more about letting loose
than letting go.

JAYNE
MAYLED
White Hot Hair

Fabulous Dyed Hair

I can totally understand all the many reasons why you may be reluctant to 'embrace the grey'. Perhaps you think it won't suit your natural colouring, or maybe you are so freaked out by the way that it signals ageing that you can't countenance the thought. There are clearly cultural pressures too. There are places where you never see a grey head of hair on a woman because the tradition is to maintain the jet-black hair of their youth. Little elderly Italian grandmothers come to mind. Then there is the ubiquitous blonde of communities of older women who can cope with a paler shade as long as it's yellow rather than white and the colour still harks back to youth and a certain kind of sexually attractive beauty. So the first consideration if you decide to dye your hair is the colour you are going to choose instead.

As children, our hair colour is the perfect balance to our eye colour and skin tone. I had mid-brown (mousey) hair, grey eyes and cool-toned skin, so I knew that as I aged I'd look fine with a combination of grey hair, grey eyes and cool skin tone. But what if you used to have dark chestnut hair, brown eyes and warm-toned skin? The temptation is to keep that rich conker-coloured hair forever. The problem is that pigment loss happens equally to the skin and, as already mentioned in the chapter on makeup, we start to lose contrast between our features and our facial skin. If you recreate a solid mass of dark hair atop a paler face in which all the main features have also faded, you run the risk of looking older because the effect is too harsh. It's deeply ironic that in the quest to avoid looking older, you'd probably look younger if you let your hair go grey, although you will no doubt hotly dispute this.

COLOUR CHOICES *to* COVER GREY

01 Firstly, don't go too dark, so avoid black or very dark brown. A cool, medium ash brown will still work with your colouring but have a much softer and more natural effect with your paler, cool skin tone.

02 A warm mid-brown with reddish tones would be a good choice if you have warm-toned skin.

03 If you are a natural blonde, it may be years before you notice the grey, especially if you have always had highlights. Grey and white blend well with blonde until the time comes when you notice that the blonde highlights look yellow in contrast to the grey background colour. Then you may need to add in both highlights and lowlights in pearl, beige and medium blonde. Cool ashy tones are best to neutralise any yellowness.

04 If you are a natural redhead your hair colour is almost impossible to imitate with dye, even though there are many shades of red you can use on your hair, from light copper to deep burgundy. Better not to cling to your natural red hair once you have more than 20 per cent of white hair. Choose a warm brown or blonde to work better with your paler skin.

Hair Length and Age

There is no doubt that, after hair colour, the second most contentious issue for older women is how long we let our hair grow. My photograph of Nicola Griffin (see right) sparked outrage because it combined grey with thick, voluminous long tresses, which is not what we expect to see on an older female. This would appear to cause discomfort at best and outrage at worst.

I wonder if this loathing of long grey or white hair dates back to medieval times? In that era people were very superstitious and believed that some older women (presumably with long white hair) had supernatural powers. They were accused of being in league with the devil and of witchcraft and sorcery and punished, sometimes by being burned to death. So maybe this is the reason we associate long grey hair with dreadful old hags. The dictionary definition of a witch includes two opposing meanings. On the one hand, you have *'an ugly or unpleasant old woman'*, but then again you have almost the opposite: *'a girl or woman who is bewitchingly attractive'*. Whichever way round you take it, it has everything to do with attractiveness. So, older women with long, sexually alluring hair in the wrong colour disrupt the natural order of things. We want that long hair to be blonde or a rich, shiny brunette or a beautiful auburn, which is no doubt why so many women start to panic the moment they spy a grey hair. With longer hair in the 'right' colour, the older woman hopes she will still be considered 'bewitchingly attractive'. The moment that long hair is naturally grey she apparently morphs from bewitching to witch-like.

Face Shapes and Hairstyles

Our faces change shape as we age because of various factors, including less fat in some areas and more in others and also the effect of gravity. To help you find the best hairstyle, take a look at your face and decide which shape comes closest to your own. There are four basic face shapes and, in order to decide which one you have, you will need a full-face photograph and a tape measure. There are four points to measure: the width across the forehead, the cheeks and the jaw and down from the hairline to jawline at the centre of the face, which will tell you the overall length of the face.

If you choose the best hairstyle for your face shape, you can create balance by minimising some features (like a high, broad forehead or a heavy, square, jowly jaw) or creating height or width as appropriate.

> **There are four basic face shapes and, in order to decide which one you have, you will need a full-face photograph and a tape measure . . .**

JUTTA

Shape One

/

A ROUND FACE

This has a similar measurement across the cheeks to the one from hair to jawline. It can look good with a short pixie crop as long as there is plenty of height on top; if not, the face will look broader. If you choose a style that is very short at the sides and back you can also create balance and length by wearing long rather than round earrings, and if you wear glasses then choose rectangular rather than circular ones. If you prefer a mid-length hairstyle (to the bottom of the jaw) then think about creating an 'A' rather than an 'O' shape with your hair. Best to avoid a solid fringe and keep the style sleek over the ears and then wider at the jaw. Shoulder-length hair will work if your neck is long enough, but again have it layered rather than all one length and have an asymmetric rather than a solid fringe.

PAULA

Shape Two

/

AN OVAL FACE

This shape has similar measurements at the forehead, cheeks and jaw but a longer measurement from hair to jawline, with rounded shapes at the forehead and jaw. You are not trying to counterbalance any particular width or length, so you can choose from a wide range of styles, including full, half or no fringe and any length that suits your hair texture. Most earring shapes will suit you and glasses will look good if they are softly rounded rectangles.

JACKIE

Shape Three

/

A SQUARE FACE

This has similar measurements across the forehead and jaw. The jaw
is decidedly strong and prominent, so your best bet is a hairstyle that
softens and adds roundness to any angularity. Avoid solid, straight,
blunt-cut fringes which would mirror the square jaw. A side-sweeping
fringe and a side parting will add asymmetry and will soften a broad
forehead, so if you prefer short hair make sure it's not a square shape
on top! Be wary of mid-length hair that ends at the jawline or adds
width at that point. It may look better to have your hair longer as it will
elongate and narrow the face. Choose button-shaped earrings to add
softness and go for gently curving rather than sharply angular frames if
you wear glasses.

Shape Four

/

A HEART-SHAPED FACE

This is broad across the forehead, often with prominent cheekbones and a much narrower and longer pointed chin. A side-swept feathery fringe can break up the forehead on a short style and focus attention on the cheekbones. A short style is best if it hugs the head rather than adding extra height and width on top. Think about creating some width at the sides with a mid-length cut rather than a straight style. Shoulder-length hair will flatter the face more if it falls as soft waves rather than being poker-straight because it will make the chin look longer. Earrings can be big and bold to add width to the lower face and glasses are best kept round or square with rounded edges to create balance.

Hair Problems: Thinning Hair

Up to now, this discussion about hair has been about choices you may want to make about colour, shape and length as you age. I have used phrases like 'crowning glory', 'lustrous locks' or 'beautiful long tresses'. There is something especially fabulous about 'big' hair when we see it framing a young and pretty face. How challenging and upsetting then for those women who, for one reason or another, experience the terrible anguish of thinning hair and possible total hair loss. We know that some men also suffer greatly when they start to go bald and spend small fortunes on remedies to stop or reverse the process, but at least no one bats an eye when they see a bald man, nor do they think he is less of a man. In fact, baldness is often associated with increased virility, while for a woman the loss of hair is associated with a devastating and almost shameful loss of femininity.

> **For a woman the loss of hair is associated with a devastating and almost shameful loss of femininity.**

The causes of female hair loss are more complex than for men. It might be down to diet, hormonal or genetic issues, or the result of illness or disease. Thinning hair is a relatively common phenomenon, with as many as 50 per cent of women over sixty having less voluminous hair than when they were younger. If the loss becomes pronounced, it can cause deep distress, so it's important to understand the causes and also some of the therapies that might help. And if the worst comes to the worst, then you might want to explore whether wigs, weaves or even hair transplants might be the best solution for you.

Main Causes of Hair Loss

There are two main causes of thinning hair, both of which can lead to total hair loss. The first, telogen effluvium, doesn't damage the hair follicles on our scalps, which means that eventually your hair will grow back. The second one, androgenetic alopecia, gradually destroys the follicles so that the hair loss is permanent. It's obviously important to determine the cause of any hair loss as early as possible so that you can take measures to slow or stop it happening if at all possible.

/ Telogen effluvium means *'the outflow of hair during the telogen or resting phase'*. It is an acceleration in the normal shedding of hair from all over the head. Each scalp hair has a life cycle of about three years and then it will shed. The hair follicle will rest briefly (telogen phase) and then start to produce new hair. This happens every day to around one hundred of our scalp hairs, so it's an ongoing process and we notice it only if we start shedding a lot of hair, especially when we wash it. There are no bald patches, just a general thinning all over the head, which usually happens around one to three months after a stressful event such as a major operation, an accident, an illness, a major life event or medication such as chemotherapy. It is also very common after childbirth and the menopause. Usually, the hair loss will slow to a more normal rate and within six months the hair should be on the way to full recovery because the hair follicles have remained undamaged. If the hair shedding persists, it may indicate an iron deficiency or an underactive thyroid gland, so it is always best to ask your doctor for a blood test to rule out any underlying problem. Of course, this doesn't make the hair loss any less distressing, but at least you know that in time the problem will resolve itself.

/Androgenetic alopecia: This is the form of hair loss that most of us (men and women) dread because it is irreversible once the hair follicles have stopped producing hair. Early diagnosis and treatment can help, however, so if you notice your parting becoming wider, get advice from your doctor and seek specialist help as soon as possible. The severity varies from a generalised thinning, especially from behind the front hairline towards the crown, to complete baldness.

The condition may be inherited and is triggered by a combination of genetic and hormonal factors which gradually cause the follicles to shrink so that the hair they produce is thinner, shorter and lighter in colour over time. It can be exacerbated by stress, as the adrenal glands secrete male androgens which cause the problem. If the follicles shrink completely they stop producing any hair. In women the process starts later than in men and usually happens after the age of fifty, when the follicles become sensitive to normal levels of male hormones in the female body. In younger women, hair thinning may be caused by polycystic ovary syndrome in which there is an excess production of male hormones. The pattern of hair loss is typically from the frontal area to the crown, while hair stays thick at the back. Therapies do exist, such as applying anti-androgens, but this is a complex condition and needs to be caught early before too much damage is done to the follicles.

/

It's obviously important to determine the cause of any hair loss as early as possible so that you can take measures to slow or stop it.

Therapies for Thinning Hair

If you are worried about the rate at which your hair is shedding then you will need blood tests to determine why this might be happening. If you discover that it is a temporary loss (telogen effluvium) with no damage to the follicles, you can expect recovery to happen over a period of several months. If, however, you have the early signs of alopecia, then you will need to understand exactly what might be causing or exacerbating the condition and then ensure that you get the appropriate remedies to slow down the hair loss. You might also find it helpful to consult a trichologist, who will have specialist knowledge and be able to offer appropriate advice.

What Can You Do Yourself?

- Seek specialist medical help as early as possible. Ask for tests to determine the cause.

- Think about your diet and whether it is sufficiently nutritious.

- If you are very stressed, seek ways to deal with either the cause or the effects of the stress.

- Thinning hair needs gentle treatment when both wet and dry.

- Look for shampoos with natural plant oils (like jojoba or almond) and it may be a good idea to use one that is labelled sulphate-free.

- Use paddle brushes with nodules on the bristles to gently massage the scalp to encourage sebum production and stimulate blood flow to the hair follicles.

- Limit heat exposure by using low settings on hairdryers and avoid curling tongs or straighteners.

Dealing With the Effects of Hair Loss

When I spoke to Trevor Sorbie, a well-known top hairdresser, about his charity My New Hair, he told me the rather shocking story of a friend of his wife who, having been diagnosed with cancer, had refused treatment because she was so freaked out by the idea of losing her hair. Few medics would be able to understand such a refusal, but it shows just how profoundly our sense of self and identity is represented by a full head of hair. However, if you do lose your hair, either for a few months after cancer treatment or more permanently, there are many ways that you can still look fabulous. I personally see no reason why you cannot be fabulously bald if you are happy to do that and you find the alternatives – wigs, scarves or hats – an unacceptable faff or too hot, scratchy or just plain uncomfortable. As I keep saying, there are no rules and this has to be a personal choice made with the support of people who love you.

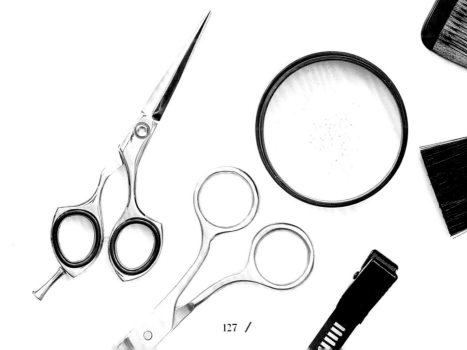

before

SUSANNAH'S STORY

Hair Loss and Regrowth after Cancer Treatment

I LOST ALL MY HAIR LAST YEAR AS A RESULT OF CHEMOTHERAPY FOR BREAST CANCER. I was a bit surprised by my reaction, which was to try to deny it, rushing out and buying a wig – which I wore only once, as it turned out. My hairdresser styled it, so that the cut was similar to my own bob, and it looked very natural, but somehow was simply not 'me'. I spent the following few months in a series of hats, scarves and turbans. My style has always been a little dramatic, so this was actually quite an enjoyable phase. The few people who saw me without headgear were supportive and, in an extreme way, it did look quite good; but it was too cold and also too much of a statement for me to feel comfortable going 'commando', as it were.

Then it started to grow back. I remember the first day I needed a hairbrush – it was a real moment of celebration! My hair was quite a nice steely grey, and I'd already decided it might be a good moment to go grey gracefully. What I was not expecting was for it to be curly! This is a side effect of the chemo which will probably wear off, but it's quite hard to accept; instead of the sleek, quite severe look I'm used to, it's a slightly frumpy mop, which reminds me of nothing so much as the 'shampoo and set' look of the elderly ladies of my childhood. Most other people like it – or say they do. I do not.

Masses of coconut oil and leave-in conditioner tames it a little bit but it's tough stuff, so sometimes, if I want to look elegant, I return to my turbans, which are at least my choice and my style. As it grows and I can find a style that suits my face, I know that I will get used to the new me, and begin to enjoy it. But it has been an interesting journey, discovering just how much my identity is invested in my hair and how important it is.

after

If the thought of exposing your balding pate to the world is too challenging then you may wish to think about some of the options you have.

HATS AND SCARVES

These can look fabulous in a head-hugging style like a bandeau or turban. I think the important thing with any option is to define the eyebrows, so that you reduce the slightly 'otherworldly' effect of a face without the usual framing we get from the brows. I came up with the idea for our Brow Shape when a close relative lost her eyebrows due to a thyroid problem, while keeping her hair and her eyelashes. My reasoning was that a portrait painter would create eyebrows by painting individual brow hairs rather than drawing a solid shape. So the LFF Brow Shape consists of a very fine brush (like a paintbrush) and a small vial of what is effectively paint. You can then put dots where the brows need to start, arch and end, and then, using light feathery strokes, you can create the most lifelike brows. The 'paint' is waterproof but easily removed with eye makeup remover.

WIGS

Wigs nowadays can look indistinguishable from the real thing. A neighbour of mine, who was recovering from breast cancer treatment, wore a wig that was so like her own hair that she had to lift the front part in order to convince me that it really wasn't her hair. I cannot write about wigs for women with either permanent or temporary hair loss without mentioning the brilliant work of Trevor Sorbie. If you decide that you'd like to wear a wig, do take a look at the website www.mynewhair.org. This charity was created by Trevor to offer excellent practical advice, in conjunction with the Department of Health and the Institute of Trichologists. It gives information on various considerations when choosing a wig, including the pros and cons of wigs made from synthetic or natural hair, and how to care for your wig once you have chosen it. Sorbie is passionate about the need to support women psychologically through their loss of hair, and about the need for wigs to be personalised to fit the individual's head and face shape. He charges nothing for his time and has created a network of over a thousand hairdressers across the UK who have been trained by him to provide, as stated on the website, 'a caring and sensitive service to their clients'. He is now taking the idea overseas.

> **The important thing is that a great hairstyle is an essential element of looking fabulous, so find one that suits your face, your 'look' and your wallet.**

As we age we have a number of decisions to make about our hair. Will we let it become the colour that nature has intended for us and wear our grey or white hair as a badge of pride rather than a sign of shameful ageing? Or will we decide to colour our hair in order to cover the grey because we feel better that way and because we think it helps us to look younger? There is no right or wrong, good or bad. Just remember to allow the colour to soften slightly as you age so that it works better with your older face. Will you grow or keep it long as an act of defiance or accept that a shorter style works better now your hair is less voluminous? Again there are no rules. The important thing is that a great hairstyle is an essential element of looking truly fabulous, so find one that suits your face, your 'look' and your wallet.

Visibly Confident

You may believe that an individual's level of confidence is fixed at an early age and cannot be improved, but I would beg to differ.

From all the emails I get from older women, loss of confidence seems to be a major component of the ageing process, which is one very good reason why I was so keen to write this book. I want it to shift your attitude to what it means to be fifty, sixty or seventy (or more) in the world today. I want you to see images that inspire you to view ageing at the very least as nothing to be afraid of, and at best as a beautiful and wondrous thing. And, above all, I want to show you how to bolster your confidence so that you can hold your head up high and say, 'I matter too.'

CLARISSA

A while ago I received this email from Clarissa Farr, who at the time was High Mistress of St Paul's School in London: *'I am 58 and have a high-profile job where I have to look my best in front of much younger people – I am headmistress of a girls' school. It's a job which can be very all-consuming. Your makeup tutorials have been brilliant to give me new ideas and new confidence with my makeup even though I'm a different generation from my fashion-conscious pupils.'*

A New Reality for Older Women

To live confident and happy lives right up to our last breath there needs to be a shift not only in our own attitudes to our ageing selves, but also in the attitudes of our ageist society. A hundred years ago women lived for around fifty-six years. Fifty years ago average female life expectancy had gone up to seventy-four. Do you remember your own grandparents – how old they looked by the time they were in their fifties? My grandmother died in 1954 aged fifty-seven and I have photographs of this little old lady who, nowadays, would be taken for at least eighty! My mum died in 1989 at the age of sixty-seven. So that makes me the first female in my matriarchal line to be fortunate to be growing properly old, but unfortunate to be doing so in a world that hasn't adapted to the new reality of what 'older' actually means.

/
BECOMING INVISIBLE

Something weird happens to women at a certain point in life. Sometime in our late forties (I blame the menopause) we become invisible to everyone except our nearest and dearest. It's as though an 'anti-ageing' plague has swept through and wiped us all from the face of the earth. No wonder women often despair as they hit fifty because it would seem to mark a point in life when the process of being considered less relevant, less attractive and certainly less employable begins. What a nonsense this is! Often we are more relevant, attractive and employable than when younger, yet we're not given credit for this. And so starts the desperate cycle of chasing a youthful appearance for fear of this terrible invisibility. We should not underestimate the impact this has on our confidence and why I am so keen to redress the balance. We need to tell our younger sisters not to despair and that life really can begin at forty. I heard the truly wonderful journalist

LADY JUSTICE ANNE RAFFERTY

ANNETTE BADLAND

Caitlin Moran (forty-two) on a *Woman's Hour* podcast the other day and, as ever, she was refreshing and engaging. At the end of the interview she said, 'I'd always presumed that if you were going to do something as a woman you would do it in your fertile years, and when your ovaries checked out, that was it – you retired to your cave to go hag. Suddenly [it seems] women have a third act. We've never had that before and it means a whole new phase for women.' Caitlin is so right, but unfortunately this fact is not recognised in the world generally and certainly not in the media. Here, the powers that be believe that, as soon as a woman reaches her sell-by date, which is set much earlier than for a man, she must be side-lined or taken out of circulation.

/

FINDING APPROPRIATE ROLE MODELS

People will point to the inimitable Dame Helen Mirren and Joanna Lumley as the wonderful high-profile role models they are. Still lovely, funny and sexy, they are the poster girls for the over-seventies. The trouble is, they are in a very small minority. So where are all the other older women who could show us how to age with verve and chutzpah? There are plenty of fabulous older women out there, being just as clever, knowledgeable and vibrant as ever; the problem is, we are not aware of their existence. A while ago I decided that we would seek out some inspirational older women in our LFF Ambassador series. I discovered that among our many loyal customers we had an Appeals Court judge, a well-known actress, and many other women who were getting on with their busy lives being quietly fabulous. So I contacted them and asked if they would be photographed and interviewed for our Ambassador series. Almost without exception they agreed, and the result is many inspirational examples of capable, productive and attractive older role models.

Why Ageism Matters

People live longer in societies (like Japan) that value and respect the older generation and encourage people to continue to lead busy and active lives long past what we might consider the natural retirement age. So how do you measure whether a society discriminates unfairly against older people? Well, a good place to start is with the language which is used, the images that are shown, and how the older generation is portrayed in television, films and advertisements aimed at their age group. For instance, most beauty companies believe (it seems to be in their DNA) that every woman must want 'eternal youth'. If you have this idea as your starting point then accepting and celebrating the ageing process is an impossible contradiction in terms. Everything that you produce, sell and promote will have to encompass the (ridiculous) notion of 'stopping the clock'.

Few people ever seem to question or challenge the term 'anti-ageing' – and yet it is the very premise on which so many beauty brands are based. With the exception, of course, of Look Fabulous Forever.

> **Few people ever challenge the term 'anti-ageing' – and yet it is the premise on which so many beauty brands are based.**

Everyday Ageism

/ Let's start with ageist language. When I had the idea for Look Fabulous Forever I had to think of a good way to attract the appropriate audience to our makeup. I didn't want to do what most beauty brands do and try to have my cake and eat it. In other words, I wanted to be able to say, 'These products work brilliantly on an older face to help to make you look fabulous.' It was important that the message was unequivocal and clear; our appeal was to women in their fifties and beyond. Also, we were not promising eternal youth but eternal fabulousness. This presented several linguistic dilemmas. I toyed with the idea of referring to our target customer as 'a woman of a certain age'. In France, this little phrase conjures up someone who is still attractive, alluring and (even) exciting – think Charlotte Rampling or Catherine Deneuve. However, I soon realised that in the UK the phrase 'woman of a certain age' didn't have the same resonance and was seen as rather twee, apologetic and coy. So I decided to bite the bullet hard and call our customer 'an older woman'. Not a 'grown-up woman' or any other pussyfooting euphemism. I also decided to turn the anti-ageing rhetoric of the beauty industry on its head and call our makeup 'pro-age'. These two decisions allowed me to be unapologetic and unequivocal. We would not talk about our makeup as 'age-defying' or 'ageless' but as 'specifically formulated for older faces, eyes and lips'. In other words, our makeup is designed to work with rather than fight against the changes we all experience as we age.

/ Airbrushed images and age-inappropriate models: Look around you at the images used in advertisements and in magazines, even the ones that know full well their average readership is well above fifty years of age. These magazines often have an older celebrity on the cover, who is usually drawn from a very narrow band of 'bankable' names. These are our 'national treasures' – older actresses and television personalities who are attractive and likeable. However, their faces are routinely airbrushed so that few visible signs of their age are apparent. Inside the magazines the ageism gets considerably worse. Most of the fashion spreads feature models who are much younger than the readership. In this way, the magazines can delude themselves that their appeal is to a wide age range, when they are fully aware that this is not the case. The problem with this approach is that we never see images that can make us feel better about our ageing face and body; nor do we get any help to imagine how we might dress in fashionable and stylish clothes. The ultimate insult is to see 'mother of the bride' fashions modelled by twenty-year-olds!

/ How does this everyday ageism affect us? I know this from the very great deal of customer feedback we receive at Look Fabulous Forever. A common thread is the fact that you are now feeling a lot more confident about yourself thanks to our videos, makeup and my weekly blogs. It's as though someone has validated you again in a way that had stopped happening. You often mention receiving compliments when you are wearing your new makeup, which means that people have noticed you, maybe for the first time in ages. You talk about getting your 'mojo' back and caring about the way you look when you had all but given up. I suppose some people might take me to task for suggesting that even in old age we should still be obsessing about surface appearance. However, I would counter this by saying that feeling much better about yourself, taking pride in your appearance (whether you are male or female), is central to good mental health and it shows a stubborn refusal to accept society's view that you are no longer of any account.

Seven Ways to Change Your Attitude to Ageing

CHALLENGE THE STEREOTYPES OF AGEING

An important way to feel more confident about yourself is by changing your beliefs about what it means to age. Research shows that thinking about ageing in terms of either decline or as an opportunity to do new things can dictate how our bodies respond. For instance, older people who hold negative beliefs about ageing have shakier handwriting, poorer memories, higher rates of heart disease and lower odds of recovering from illness. So, expose older individuals to positive messages about ageing and the result is long-term improvements in self-image, strength and balance.

ASK YOURSELF – MYTH OR REALITY?

Simply understanding how negative stereotypes affect us helps us to combat them. For instance, far from feeling more depressed, more lonely and socially isolated than millennials, people over sixty-five tend to express greater satisfaction with their relationships, financial situation, sense of belonging to a community and physical wellbeing. Research also suggests that memory and mood can be enhanced in old age. This means that the image of impoverished, mentally and physically feeble, lonely old folk is largely a myth. Having said that, if you are feeling socially isolated then think about the ways you might increase your contact with other people, preferably of all ages.

RECOGNISE STEREOTYPES IN EVERYDAY LIFE

On television older people often provide comic relief by being made to appear slightly dotty or absent minded. Or, as I have already mentioned, goods or services used by the old and infirm are usually advertised using much younger women like Linda, a model who is a slim, fit, active and very attractive sixty-five-year-old. Her modelling assignments invariably involve products like stairlifts, reclining beds and chairs and pain-relief gels! Recently, researchers examined eighty-four Facebook groups that included descriptions of people aged sixty and older. On all but one, they found that negative stereotypes predominated, with 27 per cent of the site descriptions 'infantilising' older adults and 37 per cent advocating 'banning older adults from public activities', such as shopping. Are you surprised by this level of ageism, antagonism and prejudice?

STOP BLAMING EVERYTHING ON YOUR AGE

Many older adults automatically attribute physical and health problems to ageing, rather than to specific causes that might be treatable. For example, type 2 diabetes is not caused by age but by a poor diet, lack of exercise and other factors, many of which can be addressed. Others chalk up occasional memory lapses to 'senior moments', rather than to disorganisation or busyness; in contrast, someone in their twenties who constantly loses his or her keys would never attribute that to age. Cognitive ageing is complex: there is little age-related decline in some mental functions, while others do deteriorate from middle age. However, there is much research to show that staying physically and mentally active will mitigate those losses.

LEARN TO EMPHASISE THE POSITIVE ASPECTS OF AGEING

This is all about interrupting negative thoughts about ageing and substituting positive ones. Whenever we ask our 'models' on video or photo shoots about the things they like about being older there is rarely any hesitation: 'I am more creative', 'I have more time to do what I really enjoy', 'I love playing with my grandchildren because it keeps me young', 'I feel more free to be myself because I don't care what people think about me any more'. There may be losses but there are also gains.

My involvement in Look Fabulous Forever has brought into one role everything that I enjoy most – speaking, writing, makeup and, on a daily basis, working with my team, which ranges in age from twenty-four to fifty-nine and includes my daughters. I love it all and it's come at exactly the right time.

ACCEPT YOUR AGE BUT REJECT SOCIETY'S ATTITUDE

Most people report feeling twenty years younger than their actual age, but I think it helps me to identify with my own generation rather than pretending (or deluding myself) that I am the same as someone in their late forties. I am proud of being a baby boomer and I like the way that as a group we are challenging and changing attitudes to ageing and confronting some of those stereotypes by saying, 'That's not me – I don't accept your version of who you think I am and how I ought to behave.' By being an older, successful entrepreneur I feel that I am able to show a different and unexpected business face. I am often speaking on platforms to young audiences and I love their enthusiasm and surprise at what I have achieved after the traditional age of retirement. Hopefully this affects their attitudes to what ageing means and challenges their beliefs about what is possible for an older woman like me.

BECOME AN ADVOCATE FOR POSITIVE AGEING

We can all do our bit by speaking out against ageist attitudes whenever they affect us. We can also vote with our feet by walking away until they speak to us as we wish to be spoken to. If women get sacked from prominent television posts because of their age, we can write letters of protest to the executives responsible for the decision. By 2020 there will be more people in the UK over fifty than under fifty, so we will be a very large and hopefully vocal force to be reckoned with. As a group we will also have enormous spending power and everyone will wake up to the idea that the 'grey pound' is worth something. I am ever the optimist so I believe that ageism will ultimately be eroded by the sheer weight of numbers and the realisation that 'older' doesn't have to equal beige Crimplene, elasticated-waist slacks!

'Confront some of those stereotypes by saying, *That's not me – I don't accept your version of who you think I am and how I ought to behave.*'

Creating a Confident Persona

Confidence is both an internal thought process (I am a confident person) and an external expression of how you feel about yourself (people see you as a confident person). I want to show you how to optimise both.

On a scale from one to ten, how confident would you say that you are? If your answer is a nine or ten then you don't need this section! However, if your instinctive answer is below five, then let's look at why that might be. A high level of self-confidence goes hand in hand with a high level of self-esteem. Think well of yourself and the confidence will come easily. And there's the rub. We live in a culture that doesn't like people who get too big for their boots. It also tells us that age is about mental and physical decline, with increasing frailty and failing faculties. So we really do need to challenge these ideas and make sure that we 'get a bigger pair of boots'.

> A high level of self-confidence goes hand in hand with a high level of self-esteem. Think well of yourself and the confidence will come easily.

ACCEPTING YOUR AGEING SELF

Do you despair when you look at your crow's feet and marionette lines (those lines that run either side of your mouth straight down to your chin)? Do you look at your sagging jowls and drooping eyelids and feel like pulling a bag over your head? Well that's because nothing and no one in our society tells you that all these things are not only normal but they are also perfectly okay.

To come to terms with my non-Twiggy-like body I had to stop believing that 'perfection' was a tall, slim body with pert breasts and perfect ankles. I had to start to celebrate the body I have and see its beauty as well as its flaws. I hope you will look at the photographs in this book and see that older, wrinkled faces are beautiful too. I also hope that you will see our lines and wrinkles and all other signs of ageing as a small price to pay for a life lived to the full.

BUILDING CONFIDENCE AND SELF-ESTEEM – SOME SIMPLE EXERCISES:

1/

Write down fifty (yes, I do mean fifty) things that you like about yourself. Then read them out to someone who loves you and whom you respect and ask them to say what they like about you too. Open yourself to the discomfort of this exercise and, when you hear good things from the other person, let those good things in. Please don't start excusing, denying or pushing the compliments away. At the end of the exercise, I want you to say to yourself, 'I am okay.' And that is all you need to be. You don't need to be superior or inferior to anyone else, just equally valid however different you are from them (because we are all unique individuals).

2/

Find some photographs (or videos) of you at your best. Looking really good and doing something that you are proud of having done. I have a photograph of me with my granddaughter India which helps me to acknowledge myself for the support I was able to give my daughter during India's ten months in hospital. This exercise is to write down as many sentences as you can that start with 'I am proud of myself for . . .'

3/

Write a job description for your current role in life. If you are retired you may lose a sense of worth because you have no official title. However, most women I know are still incredibly busy doing really useful things often without any real recognition.

So write down all the ways you contribute to your family and to wider society and think how much each is worth in hard cash. Give yourself a job title – like Accounts Manager if you organise all the family finances, or Senior Sales Assistant if you work in a charity shop. Now think of yourself as that person, not as someone with no salary and no status.

4 /

Ask for help if you need it. This is all about not playing the martyr. If you are feeling overwhelmed for some reason, be honest with yourself about what is happening (are you 'the strong, dependable one', for instance) and be prepared to say, 'I can't keep doing this without your help.'

5 /

Set yourself a challenge. This doesn't have to be extraordinary but it does need to be out of the ordinary for you. I am currently challenging myself daily to do 10,000 steps measured on my new Fitbit. If I have only done 8,000 during a normal day, I walk round my sitting room during the ad breaks on TV!

6 /

Value yourself enough to say no to unreasonable requests. Having trained people in assertiveness I know how important it is for women to be able to say no. If you are a people pleaser, and when you are apparently always available, it may be hard to refuse unreasonable requests, especially from family members. Value your time and your own needs enough to say no if that is what you want to do. Resist any guilt-tripping that might result and don't feel that you have to explain or justify your refusal.

FEELING MORE CONFIDENT
ABOUT YOUR APPEARANCE

I know a thing or two about body loathing. I spent most of my early adulthood feeling deeply discontented with the way my body looked. Like you, I came of age when Twiggy was seen as the ultimate role model for teenaged bodies and mine fell way short of her gawky, skinny, androgynous shape. I had generous hips and thighs and what some kind soul once described as 'milk bottle' legs. My response to the disgust I felt was to punish my pear-shaped body with continual diets which triggered periods of bingeing and even more profound self-hatred. When I see photographs of myself in my teens and twenties I am amazed at how slim I was. But I didn't feel slim and my lack of physical self-confidence blighted my early adulthood.

I have finally realised (how can it have taken me so many years?) that this is the only body I am ever going to have. It's not perfect to look at and age has wrought many unpleasant changes, making it even more full of cellulite and lumps, especially below the waist. But, you know what? I no longer give a fig. If some item of clothing in a shop doesn't fit me now, I rail against the fashion industry rather than think there's something wrong with my shape and size. I just hope that my body can be as strong, flexible, healthy and free from disease as possible. I know that if I can achieve all that for the next few years I shall be extremely fortunate. If only I had made friends with my body sooner! But it's better late than never and I am determined never to treat it with such antipathy and disdain again.

TRICIA IN 1964

TRICIA IN 1987

TRICIA IN 1985

TRICIA IN 2000

TOP TIPS

to FEEL MORE CONFIDENT ABOUT YOUR LOOKS

<u>01</u> Read the chapter on *Fabulous Style* and if you need to, get help to update your wardrobe. Make an appointment with a personal shopper in a store as this is usually free. If they pressurise you to buy something you don't like (which they shouldn't do), you can always return it. Alternatively, a style consultant can save you expensive mistakes.

<u>02</u> Learn new techniques to update your makeup. My mission in life is to help women to be happy with their older faces by knowing how to apply their makeup and what makeup to apply. Our video tutorials have helped thousands of women to look and feel better about themselves.

<u>03</u> Follow the advice on how to have *Fabulous Hair* or get help from a good hairdresser. Make sure that the colour works with your older face (if you dye it very dark it may need softening). If you have gone grey, you will also need to adjust your makeup. If your hair has changed texture and become thinner then ask about products that can help to add volume.

<u>04</u> Start exercising and eating a nutritious diet. This will help you to feel more powerful physically and more in control of your health and fitness. I started an exercise regime to get rid of my 'dowager's hump' and have started to walk tall, keep my head up and stride out with purpose. All of which makes me feel more confident.

How to Show Confidence

It's relatively easy to come across as a confident person. And I say this having trained countless individuals to do just that. Remember, people make up their minds about us in around fifteen to twenty seconds when we first meet them. So, control that initial impression. Body language is key here. Walk tall, head up, look people in the eye, take the initiative to introduce yourself, smile and don't fidget. Don't forget that how we look and how we use body language accounts for up to 80 per cent of the impression we create.

Have a firm, strong voice and initiate the conversation; try to memorise the person's name so that you can use it in conversation. I used to be brilliant at this and am now not so good. The other day I met a young journalist and immediately forgot his name. I had to say, 'I'm sorry, I haven't remembered your name.' He told me that he was Ben. So I said, 'Oh, that's easy, my son-in-law is called Ben', and from then on I remembered it. If you make something of the name exchange it can really help, so comment on the name in some way: 'Felicity? What a lovely name!' Or, 'Suzannah? Do you spell that with a "z" or an "s"?'

If we control our body language and speak confidently, that first impression will last. If we're not conscious of our age then others won't be so conscious of it either. Since I had the idea for Look Fabulous Forever when I was sixty-five, I have had to get a lot of people to believe in my vision and help me to achieve it. I have had phenomenal support from everyone who has been part of the story and not once has my age been an issue. Why? Because I am both internally confident (I am okay) and I know how to show confidence to others. Age was not a barrier to me, so it wasn't a barrier to anyone else.

Fabulous
Fitness

It is perhaps ironic that I am writing this section on fitness because I came very late to this particular party!

Like a lot of older women I have always hated exercise. As a child at school, I avoided it as much as possible. There was a truly horrible outdoor swimming pool in Newmarket where I went to school, to which we were bussed once a week in the summer term. As a pathetic non-swimmer, I spent the whole lesson in the freezing water with a white float trying to avoid the teacher's eye so that I could get away with doing the absolute minimum. We played hockey in the winter, another sport for masochists, as far as I was concerned. I usually managed to arrive well after the practice had started having 'lost' a vital piece of kit, and then spent the rest of the time desperately trying to dodge any contact with the ball in case it ruined my beautifully manicured red nails (!). Needless to say, I was never picked for any team, for which I was always extremely grateful.

Since becoming an adult I have strenuously continued to avoid anything approximating a sport or any form of exercise. I just don't see myself as sporty and I also have no physical confidence whatsoever. Unfortunately (or maybe it was fortunate), after nearly seventy years of such minimal physical exertion my body finally gave me cause to believe that I have to get off my ever-spreading bottom and get moving. I suddenly felt that a lifetime of avoiding physical activity had finally caught up with me. I realised (how can it have taken me so long?) that it's now or never – I either engage with some form of physical activity or I accept that I am on a slow slide into ever-decreasing immobility and ever-increasing painful decrepitude.

Reasons You Might Also Shun Exercise

I am not alone in my resistance to becoming a gym bunny, and all of these factors can become a deterrent to starting some kind of regime:

1/ You don't see yourself as remotely sporty.

2/ You associate exercise with something you hated as a child, like your legs turning blue on a cross-country run.

3/ You don't have the right kit.

4/ You are reluctant to 'do it' in public because you feel self-conscious.

5/ Your body is not the right size or shape for exercise.

6/ You don't look anything like the archetypal fitness fanatic.

7/ You are worried about getting changed in front of other people.

8/ You don't know where or how to start. So you don't start.

I had every single one of these objections and they represented powerful barriers to taking the first tentative steps. I persuaded myself that walking for half an hour from time to time was better than nothing. This was true, but unfortunately, as I became busier with Look Fabulous Forever, my opportunities for even this limited form of movement were curtailed.

Then I became properly unwell for the first time in years. It was 'only' flu but it pole-axed me for three weeks. Not long after that, I started to wake in the night with quite violent heart palpitations. Suddenly, my body reminded me that I actually rely on it to work properly and to stay well. The heart palpitations were terrifying – I had never given any thought to that vital organ beating rhythmically in my chest until it started to do so in an irregular and alarming way. I naturally sought medical help and, after various tests which ruled out all the possible nasties, I underwent a course of hypnotherapy. This worked brilliantly to relieve the stress which was the cause of the palpitations. However, something shifted in my consciousness. I realised at long, long last that this is the only body I am ever going to have and that I need to accept it, nurture it and get it fitter so that I can have a much healthier and more active old age than the one to which I might be heading.

> **I realised at long, long last that this is the only body I am ever going to have and that I need to accept it, nurture it and get it fitter.**

Understanding Motivation
– Why Start Exercising?

It's really important to understand your motivation because it's the key to keeping going. For me, this needs to be more than a flash in the pan; time is running out and I know that it's now or never, and every other cliché you care to cite. I am also delighted to find that I haven't left it too late. It might have been better to have started all this twenty or thirty years ago, but my body can respond and is surprising me in new and gratifying ways.

Firstly, think about what might be motivating you:

1   Your doctor has given you a health warning.

2   You are recovering from a major health crisis and/or surgery.

3   Your balance is poor and you are terrified of injuring yourself in a fall.

4   You feel generally under the weather and lack energy.

5   You groan when you get out of bed or up out of a chair and it's a long time since you could touch your toes.

6   You are short of breath with only mild exertion.

7   You would like to lose weight and know that diet alone won't shift the pounds.

8   You'd like to get out more, meet some new people and have some fun. You have heard of an interesting local group activity.

I have a personal long-term goal which I am determined to achieve in twenty years' time.

These are all good motivators but none will work in the long term unless you really understand why increasing your activity levels is important to you. If the impulse to exercise has come from a nagging relative or a bossy doctor but, deep down, you remain resistant, then it will only work in the short term. I have a personal long-term goal which I am determined to achieve in twenty years' time, in 2037. On Christmas Day that year I will be ninety years old and it will coincide with my daughter Suzy's sixtieth and my grandson Patrick's thirtieth birthdays. I want to be dancing with Patrick at Suzy's birthday party! It's such a strong image in my mind's eye and I want everyone to be saying: 'Patrick's granny Trish is ninety, you know – isn't she fabulous?!' I acknowledge that this vision of the future may be interrupted by some unforeseen occurrence, but it is largely in my hands. I have twenty years to make sure that it comes true.

CORINNE'S STORY

Why I Started Exercising . . . It all began
in my forties . . . I was healthy, happy and fulfilled. With three children just entering their teens, it simply didn't occur to me that my body would start to 'play up'.

Quite suddenly, having never had any problems, I was faced with early menopause, endometriosis and inexplicable pelvic nerve pain – everything felt awful. Over the next two years, I tried to find ways to conquer the pain, and I discovered that exercise was key to feeling a lot better. With the eventual promise of a hysterectomy, I decided to be prepared for surgery by getting really strong – I wanted to go into this fighting, and get my body back on track.

Having lost the 'Lycra habit' in my twenties, it took a lot of courage for me to get back in there. I did classes of all sorts, taking satisfaction in trying new things. My energy levels soared, and I was in much less pain. By the time I was called for surgery, in November 2009, I practically leaped onto the operating table!

The endorphins released while exercising really lift my spirits, so my body feels strong and toned inside and out. It's been a joyful journey so far, and I feel ready to face any challenges that the future might bring.

Physical Ageing

If you think of your body as a coin, health is one side of it and fitness is the other. Both are programmed to decline with age and both can be massively impacted by choices we make during our lives. You may think that physical decline is such a slow, steady and inevitable process that you might as well accept what cannot be changed. But, as I am learning, this is profoundly untrue and, even though I have come to this realisation in my seventieth year, there is still so much I can do to help my body to stay disease-free for longer. I may have left it late but I haven't left it too late, as several studies show. In fact, the older we get, the more important exercise becomes. Four consecutive years of regular exercise are enough to reap numerous benefits including reduced levels of depression, disability and cognitive problems. Not to mention healthier-looking skin and hair, and a more flexible and toned-looking body.

Our joints need to move through their full range in order to stay flexible. With limited movement comes tightness in muscles which progressively shorten. This is exacerbated by the gradual loss of muscle mass which starts from our thirties. Our lifestyle creates issues like rounded shoulders and humpy upper backs (the dreaded dowager's hump) as we sit on comfy sofas while surfing on our iPads or laptops and watching television. Sitting down for most of the day either at work or at home causes the muscles in our bottom to weaken and can also cause back pain and sciatic nerve problems, as the vertebrae in the spine become compressed. And finally, weight gain around the midriff combined with a weak core can cause the lower back to lose muscle tone and become rounded rather than ramrod straight as it once was.

A Fit and Healthy Heart and Lungs

Our bodies rely on our breath and our blood to survive. I shall never forget sitting in hospital next to my little granddaughter India before she had open-heart surgery to repair a large hole in her tiny heart. She was five weeks old and weighed less than five pounds. She was linked to two monitors: one recorded her heart rate and the other measured her oxygen saturation levels, which kept dropping because her breathing was compromised. These machines constantly triggered alarms as her small body struggled to breathe and her tiny heart battled to keep beating. She needed CPR (cardiopulmonary resuscitation) on a terrifyingly regular basis. Nothing could have been better designed to remind me how our lives hang by the thread of a single heartbeat and an intake of breath.

> **The normal adult heart is a muscle about the size of a fist with an incredibly efficient operating system.**

The normal adult heart is a muscle about the size of a fist with an incredibly efficient operating system. Its main job is to pump blood rich with oxygen from the lungs around the body, which it does more than a hundred thousand times a day. Coronary heart disease occurs as the result of various factors which cause the arteries that serve the heart to become narrowed by a build-up of atheroma, a fatty material within the arterial walls. Pain and discomfort caused by this narrowing is called angina and if a blockage occurs it can trigger a heart attack.

JANE

Women and Heart Disease

I expect you're thinking that men are much more prone to heart problems than women. But you would be wrong! There are currently around seven million people in the UK living with coronary artery disease and exactly half of them are women.

Please note: For women, heart attacks may not present themselves as the kind of severe chest pain that you may have seen on television. Women may instead have shortness of breath, nausea and vomiting and pain in their jaw and back.

> **There are currently around seven million people in the UK living with coronary artery disease and exactly half of them are women.**

Heart disease is responsible for a quarter of all deaths in the UK. Many of these deaths could be avoided with changes to lifestyle and eating patterns. A good example are the changes that have happened to the health and fitness of Finnish people over the past thirty years. Finland used to have one of the highest cardiovascular death rates in the world. Now it has one of the lowest thanks to a government initiative that sought to change ingrained habits centred on an unhealthy diet and insufficient exercise. It succeeded so well that today every city, town and village has well-lit, well-maintained paths for walking and tracks for cycling and cross-country skiing; in effect, a free, user-friendly outdoor gym.

HEART RISK FACTORS FOR WOMEN

The traditional risk factors of high cholesterol, high blood pressure and obesity affect both men and women, but there are other factors which play a bigger role for women. Here are some of them:

1/

Women with diabetes are at greater risk of heart disease than men with diabetes. It is thought that there are at least one million people in the UK with undiagnosed type 2 diabetes.

2/

Women's hearts are affected by stress and depression more than men's. Depression can make it harder to maintain a healthy lifestyle.

3/

Smoking in women is a greater risk factor than for men.

4/

A lack of physical activity is a major risk factor for heart disease. Some research shows that women may routinely be less active than men.

5/

Low levels of oestrogen after menopause pose a significant risk for developing cardiovascular disease in the smaller blood vessels.

6/

A condition called 'broken heart syndrome', often brought on by stressful situations, can cause severe, but usually temporary heart muscle failure and more commonly occurs in women after menopause.

Before You Start a New Exercise Regime

It would be irresponsible of me not to mention the importance of consulting your doctor before you embark on a new fitness regime. If you are overweight or experiencing any health issues, then you will need to know what level or type of activity is safe for you to do. However, don't make your excess weight or low level of general health act as an excuse to do nothing. As I've said, health and fitness tend to reflect each other, so as you increase your activity levels and become fitter, your general health will inevitably improve.

Tracking Progress

Before you start, it would be a good idea to assess your current state of health relative to various indicators. Some of these your doctor can do for you, such as your blood pressure, cholesterol level, body mass index and whether you are at risk (or already show signs of) type 2 diabetes. If you are concerned about osteoporosis, which can be an inherited condition and is also more likely in women who have lost their ovaries or had an eating disorder, then ask for a bone density scan (DEXA) which can give vital information for women after the menopause.

Lack of exercise can make you more likely to develop osteoporosis and exercise can help to improve your bone health if you already show some level of bone loss (osteopenia).

There are also measurements you can take at home. You can obviously weigh and measure yourself and work out your body mass index yourself. To do this, first divide your weight in kilograms by your height in metres. If you weigh 70kg with a height of 1.65m, it would be: $70 \div 1.65 = 42.42$. And then you divide by your height again: $42.42 \div 1.65 = 25.7$ – your BMI. Alternatively, find a BMI calculator online and input your height and weight.

THE GUIDELINES FOR A HEALTHY BMI ARE:

- Below 18.5 – underweight
- Between 18.5 and 24.9 – healthy weight range
- Between 25 and 29.9 – you are in the overweight range
- Between 30 and 39.9 – you are in the obese range

You can measure your waist-to-hip ratio (WHR) and work out if you are at increased risk of heart disease. This ratio is calculated by dividing the waist circumference by the hip circumference. So if your waist is, say, 101cm and your hips 96.5cm your WHR is 1.0. Any measurement above 0.85 in females would indicate abdominal obesity, which would put you at greater risk of developing heart problems.

Physical Tests

There are several different physical tests you could try, but it might be helpful to test your balance and muscle strength. To test your balance, stand on one leg with your eyes closed. You should be able to do this without putting your foot down for at least ten seconds. If you cannot do it at all or only manage two or three seconds, then take it as a warning sign of potential problems to come. And finally, test your leg muscle strength. Sit on a chair and cross your arms in front of you by holding the opposite elbow. Now see how many times you can stand without using your arms. You are aiming to stand up more than twenty-two times in a minute, preferably around thirty-five. If you cannot stand at all then, again, you are at serious risk of ill health. If you work at improving your balance and core strength, you should find these tests become easier as your general fitness improves with exercise.

How to Ensure Long-term Success

Make a note of your measurements in your fitness plan or diary at the start of any new exercise regime. I'd suggest that you also decide when you are going to check your progress. I'd counsel against constantly jumping on the scales or taking out the tape measure. I began my first steps towards a fitter future a few months ago when I contacted Lindsay Burrows (see page 172), a local fitness expert who specialises in working with older women and who takes a holistic approach to exercise which appealed to me. After just a few months I am already noticing many positive physical changes, such as improved posture when I am walking and a straighter back when I am standing, and I have lost a few pounds in weight without changing my diet. I am also sleeping better and feeling more energetic.

EASY FIRST STEPS

01 Build extra activity into each day. Since I started my 'get fit' regime, I have vowed never to drive myself to the shops or station, both of which are an easy walk from my house. This is better both for my car's engine and also for my heart! I also take the stairs at work, partly because I hate lifts. We are on the third floor and I literally cannot speak for several seconds when I get up to our office. You could try getting off the bus one stop back from your usual stop or using a car park that's further away from the shops.

02 Remember that things like housework and gardening count but on their own may not be energetic enough, especially if (which is very true for me) they are sporadic bursts of activity rather than regular daily occurrences.

03 Set yourself some goals that are realistic, attainable, measurable and time-related. Your overall goal might be to 'get fit', but this is unspecific and vague so it might not work as a motivator. Better to break your overall goal to 'get fit' into small chunks so that you don't feel overwhelmed. This could be as simple as 'walk for thirty minutes a day for a minimum of five days a week for three months'. It's important to be really clear about your motivation so that you keep going even if the going gets tough.

04 Get a pedometer, Fitbit or app for your phone. I asked my family for a Fitbit for my last birthday and have strapped it onto my wrist every morning since. I am staggered at what a difference this has made to my life. It counts my daily steps and tells me how far I have walked, how many calories I have burned in the process and how many minutes I have been active. My daily goal is 10,000 steps and I usually do at least 8,000 in an average day, as often as possible by walking in the fresh air.

LINDSAY BURROWS

Founder and Director of Me Spot

THERE'S NOTHING MORE EXHILARATING than taking the leap of faith, challenging the norm, and stepping out of your comfort zone. For me, leaving behind my comfortable yet compromised world of corporate fashion buying to start a health and wellbeing business has been an amazing ride.

Throughout my life I have met so many incredible women, many of whom juggle families, homes, careers and relationships, generally putting others before themselves. These are remarkable achievements so often overlooked, replaced instead by the anxiety of perceived inadequacies. I launched Me Spot with the sole purpose of creating an environment that encourages women to celebrate who they are and offering a set of complementary services that support them to be the best they can be. Exercise plays an important role in what we do.

Thinking back to my school days, it would have been inconceivable that I could find myself working in the exercise arena. I hated pretty much everything and, like many women, the feelings of malaise on PE day, the panic of competition and the fear that comes with having no choice, were all enduringly powerful. Then something changed.

In my twenties, on my own terms and when the time was right, I started to try some exercise classes, I went to the gym, and I began swimming. What amazed me was how good I felt afterwards, not just physically but mentally. Exercise soon became my go-to solution if I was feeling low, stressed, or if I had an important event to face at work. After exercise, what might have seemed difficult suddenly

became achievable. I would go to the gym in one mood and come out in quite another. Add the many health benefits into the mix and you have something incredibly powerful. How very different from the dark days of the bottle-green PE kit!

As a personal trainer, exercise is now an integral part of my life (although, by the way, I also still don't consider myself as sporty!) and I am passionate about helping other women to discover how transformative it can be. I specialise in working with older women and I would encourage everyone, whatever your age, to give exercise another go – the good news is, it's never too late. Rewrite the book. Leave any preconceptions behind if you can and experiment. Try different things until you find an activity you enjoy at a level that feels right for you. Look for people you connect with and an environment in which you feel comfortable. Don't be afraid to stop if you really don't enjoy it – and certainly don't see it as failure, but rather think positively and make it your resolution to find something else that suits you better. I promise, your quality of life will be enhanced, not to mention extended as a result – just ask Tricia!

Exercising the Whole Body

Before I started working with Lindsay, I associated exercise with demanding and energetic activities like aerobics, running or going on an exercise bike in the gym. While this is important, I have learned in the past few months that our bodies need different types of regular movement in order to be fully fit. I want to carry on being able to run for the train if I need to, but I also want to be able to get up easily from a low chair or the floor if I am playing with my grandchildren. I want to be able to fully turn my head when I am reversing my car. I want to be able to stand on one leg to put on a pair of trousers or tights and I also want to be able to walk long distances without tiring too quickly. In short, I need cardiovascular fitness, muscular strength in my arms and legs and core body, combined with endurance, and finally I want to have flexible muscles and joints combined with good co-ordination and balance.

Cardiovascular Fitness

This can be defined as 'the ability to take in, transport and utilise oxygen'. I've talked about the importance of the breath and the blood which is constantly being pumped around our vascular system by our heart. Cardiovascular exercise ensures that the heart, which is a large muscle, is strengthened so that it can work more efficiently. If we do regular cardio exercise, all sorts of good things start to happen to our bodies. Our resting heart rate decreases, which means the heart is not having to work so hard. The volume of blood that is being pumped with each contraction increases, to the benefit of our whole body.

> If we do regular cardio exercise, all sorts of good things start to happen to our bodies. Our resting heart rate decreases, which means the heart is not having to work so hard. The volume of blood that is being pumped with each contraction increases, to the benefit of our whole body.

The good news about cardiovascular exercise is that it's quite easy to build into your everyday life, which is a good thing because this is something we need to be consciously choosing to do every single day. In a report for the NHS on the percentage of women who spent more than six hours a day sitting down, the figures were quite shocking. For women aged between fifty-five and sixty-five it was 35 per cent on weekdays and 39 per cent at weekends; for women aged between sixty-five and seventy-four it was 51 per cent seven days a week, and over seventy-five years of age it rose to 66 per cent on weekdays and 63 per cent at the weekend. With statistics like these, there is little wonder that health problems like back pain, heart disease, obesity and diabetes escalate with age, as we become increasingly sedentary and immobile.

BEST CARDIOVASCULAR EXERCISES

WALKING: This is the one we can all build into our lives. However, we need to think about increasing what is called the 'perceived level of exertion'. A leisurely stroll is not going to cut the mustard, so we need to measure the effort on a scale that looks like this:

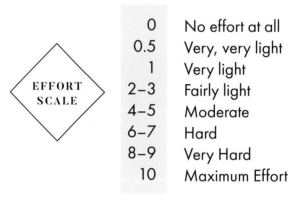

	EFFORT SCALE	
0		No effort at all
0.5		Very, very light
1		Very light
2–3		Fairly light
4–5		Moderate
6–7		Hard
8–9		Very Hard
10		Maximum Effort

In the exercise diary I have suggested you keep, note the duration of your periods of exertion. A reasonable target would be around 150 minutes of exercise over seven days. This works out at thirty minutes a day for a minimum of five days. Then you could use the RPE (rate of perceived exertion) to ensure that you have introduced the right level of effort into your sessions to make a difference. The important thing here is to work within your own limitations. It's not a competition, but it is important to be honest with yourself. To achieve significant health benefits, make a note of how hard you perceive you are working during each session as well as the time it takes, so that you can watch your fitness improve.

NORDIC WALKING: A good way to introduce increased effort into walking would be to join a Nordic walking class, a form of exercise that has considerable benefits over just putting one leg in front of the other:

1/ The poles propel you forward so that you walk faster without realising it, and as a result you get an improved cardiovascular workout.

2/ Using the poles tones and strengthens the upper body as well as the lower body – especially the back of the arms.

3/ This is a good way to strengthen the back of the arms and back. The design of the straps on the poles forces the stomach muscles to brace so that you are getting a workout for your core at the same time. It's low impact so easy on the joints.

4/ It burns more calories than normal walking.

5/ There are proven psychological benefits from being outside, and at the same time it's great fun and very sociable.

There are many other forms of cardiovascular activities to choose from, including swimming, cycling, Zumba, Jazzercise, dancing, water aerobics, tennis, squash, netball and golf. The important thing to remember is that you are looking to use large muscle groups in a continuous and rhythmic motion. This will in turn raise your heart rate, and make you slightly, moderately or very out of breath. The more you participate in these activities, the easier they become as your heart/lung capacity increases. The final benefit is that the endorphins which are released into the bloodstream as a result of exercise will lift your mood, help you to fight depression and reduce stress.

DECLINING MUSCLE MASS

Over a period of fifty years, from age thirty to eighty, we lose up to half the muscle mass we had as young, fit adults. It's known as sarcopenia and may be seen as an inevitable result of the way that our bodies decline in strength with age. But it isn't inevitable. This process can be slowed down with proper strength training, so that if you do make it into your nineties you can do so as a sprightly nonagenarian still capable of getting yourself up stairs, out of a chair and into a car.

Moving in a Co-ordinated Way and Maintaining Balance

My dad lived perfectly well at home and had a really good life until he had a fall. After a miserable year spent in a nursing home, with very limited mobility, he died at the age of eighty-one. His fall was the beginning of the end. However, as with cardiovascular fitness and muscular strength, there is much we can do to ensure that we don't start falling over and that we retain good balance and co-ordination.

Balance is the ability to keep your centre of gravity over your base of support. I mentioned the test of closing your eyes and standing on one leg. Most people can only do this for a very few seconds, but the duration can be improved with some work and daily practice. Yoga, Tai Chi and Pilates will all help with co-ordination and balance, and there are lots of individual exercises you can do on your own. Try walking in a straight line heel to toe without overbalancing. Try standing on one leg while you clean your teeth. Remember to alternate legs and keep your pelvis straight.

Flexibility

This is defined as 'a measure of the maximum range of movement possible around a joint'. As we get older, the muscles around our joints get tighter, which in turn restricts the range of the joint. Lack of flexibility makes all sorts of everyday tasks difficult or downright impossible. As I live alone, my biggest bugbear is not being able to do up a back-zipped dress or top. It's okay if I can wiggle it right up, but absolutely impossible if the dress and sleeves are a snug fit. Simple everyday tasks like washing, blow-drying and styling your hair are difficult with tight shoulders. It can also be difficult to reach things on a high shelf.

A limited range of movement in the hips, knees and spine makes getting tights on and doing up shoelaces (on your trainers!) really hard. Working on flexibility helps to release tension in the muscles, which also makes it a great way to de-stress. Loosening that tightness in the neck and shoulders from sitting too long is essential to prevent or relieve upper back pain.

Always remember to do some stretching at the end of any exercise session to release any tightness and relax the muscles. It can make a real difference if you are able to include some daily stretching into your routine, but make sure you warm up a little first.

Aim to hold each stretch for at least thirty seconds, remembering to breathe through each stretch. As you breathe out, direct the breath to the area that feels tight and, as you feel the muscle relax, gently extend the stretch a bit further.

EASY STATIC STRETCHES

/ NECK:

Stand tall with the chest open. Gently drop the chin towards the chest and feel the back of the neck lengthen and stretch. Hold. Carefully roll the chin around to one side, looking down on the diagonal and pushing the opposite shoulder down and away. Hold and then repeat on the other side.

/ CHEST:

Stand facing a doorway and place your arms at a ninety-degree angle on the doorframe. The lower part of the arm will be in contact with the frame (if your flexibility allows); the elbows will be around shoulder height. Gently push the body forward and feel the stretch across the chest.

/ UPPER BACK:

Stand tall, clasp your hands and take the arms straight out in front at chest height. Drop the chin to the chest and open up across the shoulder blades, slightly rounding through the back. Tip: try not to lift the hands too high as this can cause the neck to tense.

/ THORACIC ROTATION
(UPPER BACK):

Sit tall on a chair, making sure the spine is straight and not slumped. Keeping the head in line with the spine, twist the body around to the right using the left hand to pull against the back of the chair to help lever you around. Repeat on the other side.

/ WAIST:

Stand tall with feet hip width apart, chest open and tummy lightly drawn in. Hands by your side, gently reach down the side of one leg, taking care not to twist the body and keeping the head centred. You are moving on one plane. If your back is okay you can also reach overhead with the other arm pointing in the same direction, which extends the stretch. With this one, make sure the tummy is drawn in throughout and that you use the waist muscles to pull you back to the centre. Repeat on the other side.

/ HAMSTRINGS
(BACK OF THIGH):

Stand with feet hip width apart, knees slightly bent. Place one foot out in front of you so the leg is straight. Bend forward with the upper body and stick your bottom out behind until you feel the stretch. Take care to keep the hips square. Repeat with the other leg. Tip: doing this with the bottom against a wall can help keep the hips in the right position.

/ QUADRICEPS
(FRONT OF THIGH):

Lie face down on the floor with your forehead resting on one hand. Use the other hand to take your foot, bending your knee, and bring your foot towards your bottom. Push the thigh into the floor to feel the stretch. Make sure both knees stay together as you stretch. Repeat with the other leg.

Choosing an Exercise Class

If you are going to commit to a long-term fitness plan by attending a class, it's really important that you give some consideration to what might work best for you. So if you feel inspired to work on your fitness, here are some important things to consider when making your choice:

1 /

Do some research on the teacher's background. Ask how much experience he or she has with older exercise debutantes, especially if, like me, you really are a complete novice.

2 /

Choose a small class if possible. You may want to be lost at the back so that no one notices you, but the more individual help and support you get from the teacher, the better for your body's safety.

3 /

Tell the teacher that you are happy to be corrected and talk to them about what your personal goals for the exercise are. You need to like the teacher and be able to communicate with them and feel listened to and understood. This needs to be a two-way relationship.

4 /

Look for a programme that is not 'one size fits all' but can be adapted to your needs and pace.

5 /

If you do give up a class then don't feel guilty. Just say, 'That wasn't the right class for me' – not 'I was hopeless at that.' Try other options until you find the thing that feels right for you and which you may come to enjoy rather than endure.

Having disdained exercising and fitness for so much of my life, I am truly amazed at how everything that I have researched for this book references the benefit of physical activity in some way:

1. Want better skin and healthier hair? Then exercise will benefit both by improving circulation and bringing blood and oxygen to your epidermis, dermis and scalp.

2. Want clothes to hang better on your body? Then exercise will smooth your silhouette by decreasing unsightly bulges and improving your posture.

3. Want to lose some weight and reduce your chances of diabetes and coronary heart disease? Then reducing your calorie consumption and increasing your calorie usage by exercising is an important way to get slimmer and stay that way.

4. Want to have a healthier heart and reduce your risk of heart disease and stroke? Then aerobic activity will ensure that your heart performs its daily miracle at optimal levels.

5. Want to move more easily and keep going for longer? Then exercises will help you to lead an independent life for years to come.

And that's the real point for me. I am fiercely independent and I know that my ability to 'live the life more fabulous' would be severely compromised by physical weakness or incapacity. The truly wonderful discovery I have made after several months of exercising is that I haven't left it too late and my body loves moving more and becoming stronger. My goal of dancing with my grandson Patrick when I am ninety feels like a real possibility, and I am determined to be happily shaking my booty rather than my walking stick!

Fabulous Food

Good food is a daily pleasure, but for many women it can also be a daily challenge as they struggle to control their weight.

I can identify with this struggle because I had a love-hate relationship with food for around twenty-five years of my adult life. I became a teenager in 1960, just in time for puberty to change my body to a pear shape, which was not fashionable and which I came to dislike intensely. I gained around a stone in weight for the first time when I was at college in 1966 and so started a cycle of bingeing and starving which made me both ashamed of my lack of willpower and unhappy to be so obsessed with what I was either over- or undereating. This chapter is about the very best possible food choices to ensure that you have a long and healthy old age. If you are overweight and wish to do something about it, there are some suggestions for you to consider, but I don't want to focus exclusively on weight-loss diets but to concentrate on the best ways to nourish your body so that you are full of energy, look and feel fabulously well, and live a longer and much healthier life.

Food and Longevity

One of the best aspects of writing this book has been the research I have done into the science of ageing. How glad I am that I live in the twenty-first century! So much is being discovered about the causes of the diseases of old age, and the reasons why some people live long and active lives well into their nineties while others start to experience serious health issues from their fifties. The latest figures on life expectancy across the world are illuminating.

/
LIFE EXPECTANCY *for* WOMEN

South Korea	France	Japan
90.82	**88.55**	**88.41**
years	years	years

UK	USA
85.25	**82+**
years	years

In first place is South Korea, with an average of 90.82 years for women, followed by France at 88.55 and Japan at 88.41 years. The UK comes tenth in the longevity league table with an average life expectancy for women of 85.25 years. In the USA it's just over 82 years.

If you are wondering how you might live for the extra lease of life that is now commonplace in South Korea then read on! The South Koreans' lower levels of obesity and lower blood pressure, combined with lower levels of smoking, are significant factors in their longevity, most likely due to a diet of legumes, nuts, seaweed, fruits and dairy products. French women are also doing better than us because they tend to have slimmer waistlines and some of the lowest obesity rates in the developed world. French women living in the south of their country also live longer than those in the north, most likely because they consume a Mediterranean diet of vegetables, olive oil, oily fish and nuts. And we all know that the Japanese diet is largely based on the consumption of fish, rice and vegetables.

Modern Western Eating Patterns

There is a very good case to be made that many aspects of our modern ways of producing and eating food are contributing more to disease than to health. One statistic I have read is that over 17,000 new varieties of foodstuffs are produced every year, yet two-thirds of the calories we consume come from just four foods: corn, wheat, soy (from soya beans) and rice.

These are some of the problems for our bodies from the standard diet that many people are now eating:

1. Processed food loses nutrients in the refining process. Convenience and fast foods appeal to our taste buds but are short on nutrition.

2. Many foods now have additives, artificial colours, flavourings, chemically altered fats (called trans fats) and artificial sweeteners, which may be giving our bodies the wrong signals so that they cannot function properly.

3. Soils in which food is grown on large farms may be depleted and low in nutrients as intensive farming relies on chemical fertilisers.

4. Animals may be reared intensively in unnatural conditions and are routinely administered drugs like antibiotics.

And yet we eat processed foods greedily and in large quantities, probably because they often contain significant amounts of sugar, salt and fat, all things that make food taste the way we find most delicious.

Food manufacturers know how to ensure that we find their processed food irresistible, even addictive, so that we eat more and fill our trolleys with them when we do our supermarket shopping. Unfortunately, these foods are also most likely to add extra weight, particularly to our waistlines, and create chronic inflammation, oxidant stress and insulin resistance. It is no wonder that the older we get, the less well our bodies are able to cope with this overload of empty and potentially damaging calories.

Older Women and Weight

My intention in this book is to help you to look and feel fabulous for as long as you possibly can. I would be failing miserably if I didn't mention one of the biggest threats to a healthy and active old age – being overweight or obese. I am going to choose my words very carefully because I know what a tricky, touchy subject weight can be. GPs find it increasingly difficult to raise the issue of obesity with their patients because they tend to become quickly defensive and many are in denial about the extent of their problem. However, the statistics are alarming and are getting worse. Nearly two-thirds of men and women in the UK are obese or overweight, according to a study carried out by the Institute for Health Metrics and Evaluation. This study, which looked at data from 1980 to 2013, concluded that more people are either obese or overweight than at any time in the past three decades.

The data used in the study was based on BMI (body mass index) and while this is an imprecise tool, it's still a good rough guide. I have given the method for calculating BMI in the chapter on exercise (page 171) or you can search online for a BMI calculator and simply input your height in metres and weight in kilos. I am sure that you don't need a lecture from me if you fall into the overweight or obese category; however, I would encourage you to start making different choices when it comes to the food and drink you consume, the amount of activity you take and your attitude to your ageing self. On the next page is the inspiring story of Janet, a retired nurse, who at sixty was overweight and well aware that she was heading for trouble.

> # I have probably been on practically every known diet in my life, including the banana diet and the orange and peanut diet (don't ask!).

I am not going to advocate any one approach to weight loss because I feel you need to find something that works for you. I have probably been on practically every known diet in my life, including the banana diet, the orange and peanut diet (don't ask!), the F-plan diet, the Cambridge Diet and the good old 1,000-calorie-a-day diet. If I stuck to the prescribed food plan they all worked perfectly well to help me lose weight, and they all failed miserably to help me feel better about myself. This is why Janet's story is so relevant. Like her, I started to get a level of control over my bizarre eating habits and lose weight permanently when I began to feel happier and more confident in my own skin. If you are comfort eating or drinking then no amount of sensible dietary advice is going to make any difference. However, if you have reached a point where you are ready to say, 'Enough is enough; I want a different future', then the following sections on the very best food choices you can make will hopefully mean all the difference.

JANET'S STORY

after

IT ALL STARTED WITH YOU, LOOK FABULOUS FOREVER!

Last March I was feeling a bit sorry for myself and decided on splashing out more money than I normally spend on a set of your makeup. I'm so glad I did. After seeing an improvement in my appearance using the makeup, both because of the staying power of the product and the act of spending ten minutes each day on myself, I began to wonder what else I could achieve and to consider some proper weight loss, to see if my health improved. I've been overweight all my adult life, not hugely so, but enough to be unhealthy and depressing. I've lost and regained more weight than I care to think of over the years – Slimming World, Weight Watchers, Cambridge Diet, etc. Always lost quite well, always put it back on with interest.

I was interested to see whether there would be an improvement in my general health if I lost a decent amount of weight, as I was pre-diabetic, arthritic and suffering from IBS [irritable bowel syndrome]. I tried Dr Michael Mosley's eight-week, 800-calorie Blood Sugar Diet and went from 13 stone 5lb to 11 stone in eight weeks. I've lost a further half-stone since June, just by following the principles of low carbs, high fats and sticking to three meals a day, no snacking and not much alcohol. Christmas was easier than I thought, as I've got used to the way of eating by now and, apart from a tiny slice of Christmas pud and brandy butter and half a mince pie (oh, and too much wine!) I stuck to it. Lots of meat, veggies, cheese, cream, nuts, plenty to keep me happy. I've put on 1½lb but that will soon go.

I feel so much better! Full of energy, no more IBS, stable blood sugars and much more flexible due to weight loss, ten minutes of exercises each morning and walking 10,000 steps most days. This is what motivates me. I know that if I were to eat carbs again I would slip back and feel sluggish and disappointed in myself. As Kate Moss and I often say (we get confused for each other all the time) nothing tastes as good as feeling slim, or slimmer in my case. So keep up the good work and spread the word – it's always worth being the best you can.

before

Conflicting Advice

Do you remember when we were told that butter and other saturated animal fats were bad for us? Or when eggs were supposed to raise cholesterol and were also full of salmonella? Or that the best way to lose weight was to dramatically cut back on fat by following a high-carb, low-fat regime, by choosing skimmed milk, low-fat yoghurts and low-fat spreads? Now we are being told that this was all wrong! No wonder we are confused and somewhat bemused whenever the latest 'scientific' evidence shows that this, that or the other food is either a superfood or should be avoided at all costs. I want to cut through all this confusion and offer some sensible ways to choose foods that have a known benefit for health and longevity.

> **Do you remember when we were told that butter and other saturated animal fats were bad for us?**

When we are born we grow and thrive on only one food: breast milk. This supplies everything our bodies need to double our birth weight within the first five months as healthily as possible. Breast milk is the perfect balance of protein, carbohydrate (in the form of lactose), fat, vitamins and minerals, all supplied by the mother's body. For the rest of our lives we need a similar balance of nutrients but, unlike the breastfed baby, we have a huge range of choice over what we eat. Unfortunately, we don't always have the information and knowledge to make the wisest choices to ensure that our bodies are as healthy as possible and that we live long and well.

/
PROTEIN

Our bodies need an adequate daily supply of protein to ensure that we are supplied with the molecules necessary to make everything from hormones to strong muscles. Proteins are made up of twenty amino acids and nine of these essential amino acids can only be derived from the foods that we eat. They are essential in the sense that they carry oxygen around the body and ensure a healthy immune system. The best sources of these amino acids are eggs, fish and meat, but for vegans and vegetarians, a good way to ensure adequate levels is to eat a combination of pulses, beans and grains.

A note on eggs: These have had a very bad press in recent years and many still believe that we should limit their consumption for fear that they raise cholesterol levels in the blood. The latest thinking, however, is that it's quite safe to eat an egg every day, and that in so doing we can nourish ourselves with an excellent source of easily digested protein. Cooking alters the proteins in the raw egg, making them more easily absorbed.

/
CARBOHYDRATES:
SIMPLE vs COMPLEX

Simple carbohydrates are sugars. All simple carbs are made of just one or two sugar molecules and are the quickest and most rapidly digested of all foods. Fruits contain simple carbs, but they are also a useful source of fibre and a range of vitamins and minerals. I'd suggest you start reading food labels because sugar is routinely added to processed food and is often disguised. Look for words like molasses, corn syrup, maple syrup, glucose, lactose, fructose, maltose, rice syrup, rice extract, golden syrup, aspartame and invert sugar. These all have the same effect of a fast release of glucose into the bloodstream.

Complex carbohydrates are dietary starch and are made of sugar molecules strung together like a necklace. They are often rich in fibre and also supply us with a range of vitamins and minerals. Sources of complex carbohydrates in our diet are green vegetables, starchy vegetables like potatoes, corn and pumpkin, and pulses like peas, beans and lentils. The list also includes whole grains and the foods made from them, such as oatmeal, pasta and wholemeal bread.

> **Potatoes eaten with their skin on are a good source of fibre and vitamin C, less so when they are eaten as potato crisps.**

In addition to being simple or complex, carbohydrate sources also vary in how processed they are. Foods like fruit, vegetables, beans and grains are best eaten whole. Processing often strips many of the nutrients and much of the fibre from the food, and sugar, fat and salt may be added. For instance, potatoes eaten with their skin on are a good source of fibre and vitamin C, less so when they are eaten as potato crisps. Fruit and vegetables eaten whole are full of useful nutrients but become much higher in sugar when we drink them as juice.

The reason that a high consumption of refined carbohydrates ages us is because sugar and starch tend to give a quick and sustained release of glucose into the bloodstream. This in turn increases a process known as glycation, where glucose binds to tissues and damages them. Glycation is also linked to heart disease, stroke and chronic kidney disease. When glycogen stores are full, insulin is released to store the excess glucose as fat until the body needs to convert it back to glucose for energy.

1
FAT AND ESSENTIAL FATTY ACIDS

After protein and carbohydrates, the third essential component of nutrition is fat. Fat has long been considered the villain of the piece when it comes to treating obesity. But it seems we were misled and in fact our low-fat, high-carb diets have progressively been making us gain rather than lose weight. Fat in the diet is found in meat, dairy products, fish, nuts and vegetables, and all are important for health. The different types of fat, some of which are liquid at room temperature and some of which are solid, are made up of fatty acids, which are essential to the smooth running of our bodies, particularly our brains. There are two types of fatty acids that our bodies cannot make: omega-6 and omega-3. Both have to be sourced from our food. Omega-6 is relatively common and our main source is vegetable oils, which are widely used in food production (again, read the labels!). Omega-3 is rarer and is mostly found in three sources: beans, oily fish like salmon and mackerel, and in grass-fed animals that eat a diet of omega-3-rich grass and clover.

The importance of omega-3 cannot be overstated for brain function and health. Our brains are made up of 50 per cent fat and half of that is derived from omega-3 fatty acids. Low levels of omega-3 are linked to depression and anxiety. Both omega-3 and omega-6 are vital for life but need to be in balance, and the modern Western diet tilts us to more omega-6 than omega-3. To keep your omegas in balance, increase your consumption of omega-3 foods like oily fish and eat unprocessed foods like seeds and nuts for omega-6. If you then reduce your consumption of crisps, biscuits and other snack foods, you will lower your overall intake of omega-6 because these foods are often cooked in vegetable oils.

VITAMINS AND MINERALS

By eating a wide and varied diet we will ingest most of the nutrients we need to stay well nourished and healthy. However, we also need to be aware of the role that small amounts of vitamins and minerals play and the ways in which they contribute to longevity, both for their antioxidant properties and various other health benefits. The first is calcium, a mineral essential to bone health which cannot be made by the body. We are constantly rebuilding our skeleton so we need a daily supply, and this needs to increase with age as we lose our ability to repair our bones so efficiently. Milk is the most obvious source but so is yoghurt. Eating 2 X 175mg pots of yoghurt a day will supply half your daily calcium needs. However, we need vitamin D to be able to absorb the calcium from our food. We get vitamin D from exposure to sunlight, so a supplement may be useful in the darker winter months spent indoors.

> **We need to be aware of the role that vitamins and minerals play and the ways in which they contribute to longevity.**

Vitamin C from fruits like kiwis, strawberries and oranges is another vital element for the wellbeing of our blood vessels and skin. There are also eight different types of B vitamins, found in a range of natural foods. Vitamin B6 is found in nuts and does everything from keeping the nervous system running to processing amino acids into the proteins we need to repair muscles and organs. Avocados, eggs, salmon and green vegetables all give us vitamin E, which acts as an antioxidant and protects from the damaging chemicals formed when we extract energy from food. Vitamin A from carrots, peppers, plums and berries keeps our eyes healthy and helps us fight infections.

CHANGING OUR RELATIONSHIP
WITH FOOD

Whenever I read articles about the latest food fad, whether it involves chia seeds or something like kale and ginger smoothies, I feel like reaching for a hugely calorific scone piled with butter, jam and double cream! The advice always seems to come with a whiff of moralising condescension which I find profoundly annoying. So I really don't want to do the same thing here, but I may come across with a touch of missionary zeal because I have realised, rather late in the game, that the food I consume between now and my final breath is a) entirely in my control as I both buy and eat it myself, and b) one of the main factors in how long I will actually live. My biggest problem is my very sweet tooth. As a postwar child born in the countryside, I was lucky to eat a diet of good home-grown fruit and vegetables, but my mum made delicious cakes and puddings and we ate those every day too. I still feel deprived if I don't have a daily sweet treat.

LEONIE WRIGHT

I DECIDED TO SORT OUT MY HEALTH ISSUES without the support of medication. After having been on high blood pressure medication for fourteen years, I was diagnosed with high cholesterol eight years ago. Not having been comfortable with taking medication in the first place and now being prescribed statins [which lower cholesterol levels but can have side effects such as muscle damage, dementia, heart failure and more] it was time for a change.

Researching other ways of reducing my blood pressure and cholesterol, I came across a six-week cleansing programme in

Holland, my native country. After completing the programme, both my blood pressure and cholesterol reached healthy levels and I no longer needed medication. This has stayed the same since. After this life-changing experience I negotiated a UK franchise, trained as a nutrition coach and qualified in nutritional awareness.

Since May 2010 I have run my own business, EatWright, based on the Dutch programme. I work with people suffering from type 2 diabetes, high blood pressure and cholesterol, and other health issues. An additional benefit of my programme is long-term weight loss: on average clients lose 5–8kg in six weeks but, more importantly, sugar cravings and addictions disappear.

I am on a mission to scrub refined white sugar from your diet! I am a firm believer that we are what we eat and that nourishing ourselves with nature's food is the key to enhancing our health, vitality and state of mind. Mostly, our bodies can heal themselves if given the right foods, and a healthy diet generates benefits in every area of our lives.

FABULOUS FOODS *for a* LONGER, HEALTHIER LIFE

01 **Salmon:** Everything I have read about the subject of food and ageing mentions the benefits of eating salmon. It's our best bet for those vital omega-3 fatty acids and also selenium, vitamins D and E and calcium.

02 **Oily fish:** Like salmon, sardines, mackerel, fresh tuna and herring are also great sources of omega-3 and have an anti-inflammatory effect that combats arthritis, and helps to reduce the risk of type 2 diabetes and prevent insulin spikes.

03 **Pumpkin seeds:** A good source of zinc, calcium, iron, B vitamins, phosphorus, potassium and omega-6 and omega-9 fatty acids. I've started sprinkling them on my breakfast yoghurt. Delicious!

04 **Chicken:** Remove the skin and this is an excellent source of lean protein. It is also one of the best sources of zinc, needed for a healthy immune system and libido, and fully functioning thyroid.

05 Yoghurt: As we age we may find it harder to digest food. Plain yoghurt is helpful for boosting the immune system and the beneficial bacteria in yoghurt can help us to absorb calcium, magnesium and iron. The Lactobacillus bacteria help to reduce cholesterol in the blood. Low-fat varieties will most likely have added sugar.

06 Oats: Get your oats from porridge, oatcakes or oat bread to boost energy levels and supply you with B vitamins. Oats are also a useful source of beta-glucan, a soluble fibre which can reduce cholesterol. Eating 3g of beta-glucan has been shown to reduce cholesterol by 10 per cent over three months.

07 Tomatoes: These are rich in vitamins C and B5 and contain lycopene, an excellent antioxidant that also helps to prevent skin damage from UV exposure. Lycopene can also promote prostate health and is most easily absorbed after heating, so tomato purée and even tomato sauce are a great choice as well as fresh tomatoes.

08 Broccoli: It's best to steam broccoli as boiling reduces the concentration of glucosinolates, which have been shown to kill tumour cells. This vegetable is a good source of vitamin C and magnesium, which may become depleted as we age.

09 Walnuts: These contain the highest levels of omega-3 fatty acids of any nuts. They are good for strengthening artery walls, which helps to prevent heart attacks and strokes. Eating just a handful of walnuts weekly has been shown to have several benefits, including reducing cholesterol and increasing vigour.

10 Avocados: High in antioxidants and vitamin E, avocados are also rich in oleic acid, a monounsaturated fatty acid which has been shown to lower cholesterol. They can help protect the skin from free radical damage and can help to hydrate the dry skin of which many older women complain.

11 Garlic and onions: Garlic eaten with as little cooking as possible is helpful in controlling damaging levels of homocysteine in the body, and onions are a rare food source of chromium, a mineral that enhances the action of insulin.

12 Extra virgin olive oil: Like avocados, olive oil is rich in oleic acid, which is a monounsaturated fatty acid. Extra virgin olive oil is rich in polyphenols and antioxidants, which help to lower cholesterol and the risk of heart disease as well as protecting us from free radical damage.

This is clearly just a small selection of the very many foods that supply the kind of nutrition we need to keep our ageing bodies healthy and also to keep damaging chronic conditions like type 2 diabetes and rheumatoid arthritis at bay. I have always viewed food through the lens of weight loss rather than longevity, so the study I have undertaken for this chapter has been a real eye-opener. I ran a slimming club from 1974 until 1986 and helped many women to lose weight and feel better about themselves. The diet I recommended then was based on calorie-counting and included many of the foods mentioned here – things like chicken, fish, salads and vegetables. The main difference is our changed attitude to the importance of good fats in the form of foods like extra virgin olive oil, avocados, nuts and seeds, and understanding the dangers of blood sugar spikes.

If I were running a slimming club for women over fifty-five today, I would advocate a weight-loss plan that worked to lower and stabilise blood sugar, because it is very obvious that subjecting our bodies to continual peaks and troughs of glucose is damaging to our waistlines, energy levels and general wellbeing. It's also shortening our lives. This is shown in the higher life expectancies of people who live in countries where a predominantly Mediterranean diet based on vegetables, olive oil and fish is consumed, as opposed to a standard Western diet based on processed foods, refined carbohydrates and red meat.

Since I started exercising, I have felt so much more connected to my body that I have also begun to change the way I am eating. I have definitely lost a few pounds in weight, nothing dramatic, but my tummy is smaller and I feel more svelte, which may be partly down to the specific exercise regime I have followed. I am also convinced that the Fitbit is working brilliantly to make me less sedentary. I am undoubtedly much more active every day than I have been for years.

Water is Vital for Life

Liquids, especially plain water, are more immediately important to our bodies than food. We can live for about three weeks without any food whatsoever, but we would die within about three to four days without fluids. Water improves our skin, helps us to concentrate better and can also help us to lose weight by making our stomachs feel more full. I keep a large glass of water by my bed and drink it before I get out of bed every morning. This helps to rehydrate me and wakes me up.

The problem with drinking the recommended two litres of water a day is that we need to go to the loo more frequently, and we all know what a challenge that can be! Like a lot of older women who have given birth, albeit over forty years ago, I suffer from 'urge incontinence', which just means that when I need to spend a penny, I have to do so as quickly as possible. I like to keep myself hydrated, not least to prevent headaches, so I am meticulous about ensuring that I avail myself of the facilities wherever I am. In other words, I never think, 'I can wait until I get home', because the discomfort and stress of worrying about 'being caught short' is too great. Many older women are very dehydrated because of this fear and I can often feel the dehydration in their skin when I am doing a makeover.

Alcohol

The best thing for me to do here is to give you some general advice about alcohol because I have no personal experience of drinking it. I am one of those weird people who never acquired the taste, mostly because of a sensitivity to something in alcohol that triggers vicious migraines. This has deprived me of the benefits of alcohol as an enjoyable and pleasurable part of social life (especially in our society), but it has also meant that I haven't experienced any of the downsides either. From a healthy ageing perspective, drinking fourteen units of alcohol a week is the recommended limit for women, which means drinking seven medium-sized glasses of wine a week. If you are regularly drinking more than the equivalent of seven glasses of (preferably red) wine a week, then you probably don't need me to tell you that your alcohol consumption will impact negatively on your health and waistline.

Coffee

Drinking three to four cups of good-quality coffee a day may have several beneficial effects, from improving mood and increasing energy levels, to reducing the risk of liver disease, cognitive decline and melanoma. Coffee also contains useful antioxidants. In one trial on coffee, researchers tested whether coffee might improve the health of forty people with chronic liver disease. Half the group drank four cups of coffee a day and the other half drank none. After a month, the coffee drinkers had lessened the oxidative stress in their blood, which can have positive health benefits. Just remember that adding sugar and milk or cream increases the calorie value and delivers that sugar very rapidly to your bloodstream. Also, if you are a strong-coffee junkie and drink many cups a day then you will be overstimulating your adrenal glands and creating extra stress on your body.

Drinking three to four cups of good-quality coffee a day may have several beneficial effects.

CHANGES I HAVE MADE TO MY DIET:

1/

I used to start my day with toast and jam with a low-fat spread. My breakfast now consists of fresh fruit, nuts, seeds and whole Greek yoghurt. With it, I drink unsweetened tea with milk.

2/

At lunchtime I was fond of Ryvita spread with butter and topped with goat's cheese and caramelised onion chutney (yum). Now I eat either a huge mixed, colourful salad with chicken, salmon or mackerel, egg or avocado, or a big bowl of vegetable soup if it's a really cold day.

3/

I have started eating a lot more fish rather than the red meat I would invariably choose for my main meal in the evening. I now eat fish at least five times a week, accompanied by a range of vegetables. I make sure I eat at least three portions of oily fish a week, either for lunch with a salad or in the evening.

4/

I have (almost) completely cut out chocolate because it makes my acne rosacea worse, but I still have two treats a day to satisfy my very, very sweet tooth – a small piece of cake with a cup of tea at 4 p.m. and a choc ice which I eat most evenings as a dessert after dinner.

5/

I have increased the amount of water I am drinking and try to have drinks of water regularly throughout the day.

I hope you haven't read the chapters on exercise and food thinking that I am a killjoy and also too good to be true. I have struggled with food, weight and body loathing for years of my life and I regret the waste of time and energy when I could have been doing something more creative and satisfying. I have started to exercise for the first time in decades and can already feel the benefits in my posture, strength and flexibility. I have lightened the glycaemic load in my diet by eating fewer sugar-rich processed foods and my body is responding positively with some weight loss and more energy. I have also realised that food is mental nourishment too. Good, delicious food of the sort listed in the Fabulous Foods section (page 202) eaten slowly and mindfully can be points of pleasure in my day rather than rushed grabs of something filling consumed while standing at my kitchen counter. I really want to age as slowly as I can; I want to stay disease-free for as long as I can and not have to take loads of pills every day for this or that ailment. I also want to be able to do everything on my 'still to do' list. And the truly wonderful discovery I have made is that I haven't left it too late. It doesn't matter when you start to take yourself in hand as long as you begin somewhere and commit to it.

'I really want to age as slowly as I can . . . I also want to be able to do everything on my "still to do" list.'

Living the Life More Fabulous

The wonderful thing about being older in the twenty-first century is that we have so much more life to live fabulously!

However, as a society we haven't yet caught up with the idea of what it means to live a very long life. We still think of the third act of our life as a period of 'retirement', and we still tend to think of it as a time of winding down and withdrawal from the world before we pass on to whatever comes next, either eternal oblivion or eternal bliss (we hope). In which case, of course, we will have no need of a fabulous new look with our makeup, hair or clothes. We needn't worry about how well our bodies are ageing and whether we need to pay attention to our food and nutrition or our activity levels. It doesn't matter whether we feel strong and confident to go out into society and engage with it on our own terms as this older but still vital person. Because, according to the 'withdrawal' narrative, we are now invisible, irrelevant and have come to the end of our useful life, so we can rest our weary bones and wait for the end.

Renaissance and Renewal

All of that may have been true for our grandparents and possibly our parents, but it doesn't fit the bill any more because most of us will have twenty or thirty years to live after our 'official' retirement. I have no intention of becoming invisible, irrelevant or twiddling my thumbs while I wait for the end. So, instead of accepting this gloomy and pessimistic appraisal of what ageing means, it's up to every one of us to challenge the assumptions of what is possible for all us oldies. Instead of so-called retirement, I'd like to see this time described as a period of

renaissance and expansion rather than contraction and winding down. Then it becomes a wonderful opportunity for growth and an exploration of possibilities and pastures new, whether they be physical, mental, emotional or geographical. If we turned the old assumptions on their head, we could create a whole new road map full of exciting, unexplored pathways signposting us through this last great adventure of a life fully realised and well lived right up to the very end. Then we really will need a vibrant lippy, some jazzy new clothes and a smart new hairdo to go with our confident attitude, and a body and mind fit enough to carry us forwards into this fabulous future. In this chapter, I want to look at all the ways we can ensure that this renaissance can happen.

Living a Life With Few Regrets

I realise that most of you would rather not contemplate your own demise, but just for a moment, imagine you are on your deathbed – what would you regret most about the life you have lived? What might you wish you had done more or less of? In 1989, when I was forty-two years old, I had the privilege of spending three weeks with my mother who knew she was terminally ill and would shortly die. The melanoma that had begun as a malignant mole on the back of her leg ten years previously had now spread to become liver cancer, and was going to end her life at the young age of sixty-seven. You may think that this

> **In order to die with few regrets we must keep living fully until the moment that our bodies can no longer keep going.**

was a terrible and distressing time, but my mother was an exceptionally strong, brave and forthright woman. Once her intense pain was under control, she and I were able to enjoy her final days of life and to say all the important things that need to be said between two people who love each other. She taught me that it is possible to have a good death. She also made me realise that in order to die with few regrets we must keep living fully until the moment that our bodies can no longer keep going. Her death had a galvanising effect on me. I remember thinking, 'I may only have twenty-five years left if I die at sixty-seven like my mum. I mustn't waste a moment of that time.'

The second time I had such a powerful sense of 'carpe diem' was at the age of sixty-five. I had been working as a management training consultant for around thirty years, first with a large international consultancy, and then in my own business which I set up in 1996. This in itself had been a risk, but I knew that I wanted autonomy and flexibility in my working life and decided that I could make it work, especially as my clients were very loyal to me. The gamble paid off and my business did very well, allowing me to be financially secure with a good pension and mortgage-free by my mid-sixties. At that point, I had no great sense of moving into a different phase called 'retirement' and gave little thought to 'what now?' or 'what next?' Then, as I have detailed in the introduction, my fourth grandchild India was born with a rare chromosomal abnormality and complex physical needs. For her first year of life we pulled together as a family to offer support and I was more than happy to put my life on hold to do whatever was needed both as a mother and grandmother. When the crisis of India's survival had passed and we all adjusted to the new reality, everyone else seemed to be getting on with their lives. However, I felt that I had no life to resume! Fortunately this existential crisis was just what I needed to inspire me to get off my sofa and out into the world to create a whole new business and a whole new sense of purpose and direction.

Looking back I realise that, after India's first year of life, I was in the same boat as many are at that moment when their third act of life has started. We think we know what retirement will look and feel like, but only as an absence or as a 'freedom from something'. We know that there will be an absence of work, salaried income, job status and identity. There will be less structure to time and less pressure to perform or behave in a certain way. There will be fewer expectations about appearance and conformity to rules and there will be oceans of time to fill. All of which can be seen in one of two ways: as a welcome

> # It may seem strange to talk of ambitions, aims and goals but that is exactly what we may need if we are to stay vital, purposeful and engaged in the world.

retreat from engagement with the world of work and a well-earned right to play golf (or watch daytime TV) every day, or as the most fantastic opportunity to reinvent yourself and do all the things that, on your deathbed, you'd regret not having done. One question to ask is: 'What am I living for?' It may seem strange to talk of ambitions, aims and goals but that is exactly what we may need if we are to stay vital, purposeful and engaged in the world. Ultimately, this could prolong our lives and make the life we do lead very much more satisfying and fabulous.

SPRING-CLEANING OUR ATTITUDES

When we are born we are *tabula rasa*, or a clean sheet of paper. Life writes its story for us and our personality and behaviours take shape. We learn to live in the world according to a set of beliefs and perceptions about who we are and what we are capable of achieving. As we enter this third stage of our life, we may need help to confront and challenge some of this old clutter. For very many women, the overriding need may be to stop feeling guilty about putting themselves first or saying no to unreasonable requests. It might be about learning to become assertive rather than submissive, aggressive or passive-aggressive. When I decided to start Look Fabulous Forever I knew that if it was successful I would have much less time to spend looking after my grandchildren. I balanced this in my mind by thinking that it would also mean that I wouldn't be so emotionally dependent on my two daughters. As it has turned out, the business now employs both daughters, and my grandchildren think it's really cool to see Granny in the newspapers and occasionally on TV!

Unhelpful Attitudes

BEING A GRUMPY OLD WOMAN

A while ago there was an amusing TV programme called *Grumpy Old Women*, in which various well-known older celebs could bemoan aspects of the world in an amusing way. Some older people seem to feel an entitlement to moan about and criticise everything and anything they see around them, as if they know better than anyone else what is right and proper. The language they use is full of 'shoulds', 'oughts' and 'musts' and is very wearing. Being older does not automatically confer rights over and above the ones we would give to anyone, regardless of age. If you are on a high horse, I would suggest you may need to climb down from it and start seeing things from different perspectives.

BEING PESSIMISTIC

You may also believe that this is fixed – you are either a glass-half-full or a glass-half-empty kind of person. This in itself is a pessimistic conclusion. It implies that change isn't possible and that it's futile to try anything new. If I had been a pessimist, I would never have started Look Fabulous Forever. On paper, there was little about my business idea that made sense. I was proposing to sell makeup to older women online. But, according to research, older women don't buy much makeup, can't use the internet, not many watch makeup tutorials on YouTube, and anyway older faces don't need specially formulated products. I actually met a man who worked in the beauty industry the weekend before I launched the business and he said very patronisingly, 'You realise this won't work, don't you? Only the young are interested in makeup and if this was a good idea, the beauty industry would already have done it.' I just thought, 'I'll show you!' Optimism lets you take risks, helps you to look forward rather than back and literally prolongs life.

BEING FEARFUL OF
THE MODERN WORLD

The other day I climbed into a black cab in London. I was late for a talk I was giving and the cabbie asked me why I was in such a hurry. He then asked me what my talk was about and I told him that, as the founder of an online retail makeup company for older women, I was speaking about starting a new business at the age of sixty-five. Then he said, 'Can you do all that techie stuff, then?', and I said that, yes, it had been challenging, but I had mastered all that was needed to run the business. To which he replied, 'I can't even send a text and I won't have a mobile phone – I hate the modern world and just wish we could go back to how it was when I was a child.' He was sixty-five years old and blamed the world for leaving him behind. The world doesn't care about us; it just keeps turning on its axis and we either adapt and survive or we become dinosaurs, wondering why the terrain has become so inhospitable. If we want to engage in a meaningful way with the present and the future we need to adapt to it and learn the language that is now being spoken there.

AGE-RELATED BELIEFS

This can strike at any age in our life. Even as children we are being told that such and such an attitude or behaviour is no longer appropriate 'at our age' – and I bet you minded when your parents threw your dummy (pacifier) away and told you that you were a big girl now! All our lives we have been storing ideas about what an old person is like. We may have watched our grandparents as they have aged. My maternal grandmother looked like everybody's idea of a little old lady, despite being in her fifties when she died. My father became a grumpy old man and refused to go anywhere further than about two miles from home from the age of seventy until he died at eighty-one. But my dad was born a hundred years ago and lived through a very different era from me, so his experience can tell me very little about how to age now. There were a myriad of reasons why it was a crazy idea to become an entrepreneur at the age of sixty-five, but I honestly believe that it was the perfect age to do it. This is what I mean about there being no road map. Ageing in the past is not the same as ageing now. We are healthier, fitter and stronger and, hopefully, more open-minded than the last generation. We also grew up at a time of relative peace and, as a generation, we have been responsible for great social change. Now we need to do the same with ageing.

THE OTHERS IN YOUR LIFE

For most of our lives, trying new things and taking new directions will be applauded and encouraged by our friends and families. They will (hopefully) be delighted by the idea of you doing something new, even if it's a bit dangerous and risky. But will they be so enthusiastic if you suddenly announce that you are going to move to the other side of the country, run your first marathon, start internet dating or put all your savings into a new business at the age of sixty or seventy? I think it depends quite a lot on how much it will affect them and what their own attitude to risk is. If your nearest and dearest find fault with your plans, you may need to dig deep and think about why they might be objecting.

FEAR OF FAILURE

What if it doesn't work out? Do you remember that book called *Feel the Fear and Do It Anyway*? I seem to remember it started with the words: 'The only thing we need to fear is fear itself.' I'd ask yourself: 'What's the worst that could happen?' Obviously, if the answer is, 'I might die', then you may need to think again. However, most of the risks I want to explore with you will not be life-threatening but life-enhancing. You may need to think of the worst-case scenario and how you would cope if it happened, but that's just being sensible rather than overly cautious. Fear of success can also hold you back if somewhere in your subconscious you don't think you deserve to have what you want or that you can't possibly 'live the dream'.

CAROLINE'S STORY

MY LIFE OF ADVENTURE and physical challenge began aged forty-five in 2003. I did the MoonWalk, an overnight marathon walking around central London in a specially decorated bra, in memory of my dear friend Andrea. It was an amazing experience to be with 15,000 like-minded souls, and I felt a huge sense of achievement having raised a couple of grand! Having got the fitness bug, in 2004 I organised a team to do the London to Brighton bike ride for the British Heart Foundation and then in 2006, I saw a BHF flyer advertising a three-and-a-half-day Inca Trail trek. Having wanted to visit Machu Picchu for around twenty years, I decided to raise funds for the BHF and a colleague's baby who'd undergone heart surgery at the age of three weeks. This raised around £4,000 and I met some lifelong friends.

In 2008, I completed the BHF Three Yorkshire Peaks challenge, accompanied by many of my Inca Trail buddies. The same year, I did a 160ft bungee jump in St Thomas' Hospital car park, again for the BHF, and then undertook a skydive sponsored by Nivea for a product launch. What an amazing experience to leap out of a plane at 10,000ft with a man strapped to your back! And not just any man

– he was the double for Bridget Jones in the famous parachute scene in *The Edge of Reason.* This is something I would definitely do again! In 2009 I was ready for Everest Base Camp (5,545m), a twelve-day trek. Sleeping in tents at -20°C was very challenging, as was coping with 50 per cent less oxygen, but I met and made made more amazing friends and raised £5,000 for the BHF.

In 2010 I trained for seventeen weeks and ran a half-marathon for Beating Bowel Cancer. In 2011, for a local medical charity, I rowed 21.6 miles up the Thames in the Great River Race in a storm of biblical proportions, with the team raising £6,000, and then later that year ran two 5k events for the Victoria Foundation and Race for Life. I also slept rough overnight on the banks of the Thames for Action for Children to help stamp out homelessness among young people, and our team again raised £6,000.

In 2013, I abseiled down Battersea Power Station while dressed as Catwoman for Cancer Research, and then I did a 10k run with the autistic son of a friend with whom I had such fun preparing. In 2014, I had a quiet year with just a 5k run for the BHF around Regent's Park, and in 2015 I completed the 20-mile overnight Pink Ribbon walk for breast cancer. In 2017, I managed the ascent of Mount Toubkal (4,167m) in Morocco at my second attempt, having been snowed off in 2013. So this time it was all about meeting up with some of my Inca Trail buddies of ten years ago, having fun and getting to the top.

What I love about my adventures is that they give me a chance to reconnect with myself and to meet amazing people and make wonderful friends.

Deciding What You Want

I've already suggested that a good place to start your renaissance (as opposed to your retirement) is with two questions about this last part of your life:

1/ What would be my biggest regret on my deathbed?

2/ What am I living for?

These are not trivial questions and may be very difficult to answer, so don't feel you have to know right away. Just asking the questions might throw up some interesting thoughts and surprising ideas. In this section, I want to talk about risk-taking and challenging yourself, which sounds quite terrifyingly as though I am going to suggest climbing Mount Kilimanjaro or taking up skydiving or doing the Cresta Run on a bobsleigh. None of which would remotely appeal to me, although they may of course appeal to you!

Will you take the road less travelled or settle for the safety and security of sticking with the same old, same old? Which would you regret most on your deathbed: not doing it or doing it and risking failure – or success?

RISK VERSUS SECURITY

People often tell me how lucky I am and I would agree that I have experienced a great deal of luck in my life. However, I tend to think of myself as fortunate rather than lucky because I am one of those annoying people who thinks we create our own luck. There is a saying that 'fortune favours the brave', and I do think that being a bit braver and less cautious is really key if we are to live the life more fabulous. Here are some of the risks I have taken:

1 /

At thirty-four, to study for a BA honours degree when I had young children.

2 /

At thirty-eight, to telephone the head of a management training consultancy and ask for a job.

3 /

At forty-two, to leave my marriage of twenty years.

4 /

At forty-eight, to buy and restore an uninhabitable, ruined property in France.

5 /

At forty-nine, to start my own training consultancy.

6 /

At fifty-eight, to bid at auction for a flat in London.

7 /

At sixty-five, to start a new business.

The subject of risk-taking is an interesting one for all of us third-agers, because in many ways as a group we are all taking the road less travelled, which was ever the riskier option! Of course, many others have lived to a great age, but they have never done so in the clear expectation of doing it. For the last generation, ageing was seen as either a shorter or longer time in 'God's waiting room'. You had come to the end of your useful productive life, so best to withdraw gracefully, make few plans and expect senescence. When we mentally adjust to the idea that our lives will very likely last for a minimum of twenty or thirty years after our official retirement age, we can fully open ourselves to the opportunities that might present themselves for us to explore. This will require that we engage with the concept of risk as it might apply to us now.

Life is a series of calculated risks. Even walking out of the house we run the (albeit remote) risk of being killed, but we probably figure that the alternative, which is never leaving the house, makes that risk worth taking. But what about the risk of making a change or taking a chance on something you have always wanted to do – what then? Will you take the road less travelled or settle for the safety and security of sticking with the same old, same old? Which would you regret most on your deathbed: not doing it or doing it and risking failure – or success?

Dare I say that risk is a great topic for women in particular. I often used to run development courses for females at various levels of management. Many of these women had seen their less competent and less experienced male colleagues apply for more senior posts while they, despite being very capable, waited cautiously until they felt totally qualified for the more demanding role. Why does this happen and how can we change our attitudes to the possibility of putting ourselves on the line and embracing the harder, scarier and riskier option?

WHAT STOPS US TAKING A RISK?

/ We overestimate the probability of something going wrong. This is the essence of the overcautious approach. So paralysed are we by the what-ifs that we never actually commit to the change we want to make or the chance we want to take. Nearly twenty years ago, I took the risk to buy a ruined cottage and barn on six acres of land in France for twenty thousand pounds. It was uninhabitable and had no running water, but it did have something priceless: a spectacular view over a wide valley. You would not believe the number of what-ifs people came up with. What if you can't get planning permission? What if the French builder rips you off? What if you don't find a water source? What if the costs escalate and you can't afford to finish it? And so on! At the time I was single, so there was no strong male to deal with the builder (!) and I was working full-time, so I had to manage the project from the UK. And you know what? None of the what-ifs happened. My brilliant French builder built the house and pool in twelve months at the agreed budget. He drilled for and found a good water source which ensured planning permission. I was lucky – or was I more accurately fortunate?

/ We catastrophise the probability of something going disastrously wrong. So the what-ifs lead to a thought process that spirals down into: '. . . and then I will lose everything and be destitute and end up as a bag lady on the streets and then I will die a horrible lonely death'. Really? Could that really be the consequence of your risk-taking? I once decided to buy a property at auction having spent rather too long watching *Homes Under the Hammer* on television. I noticed, as I was driving past, a 'For Sale by Auction' board outside a ground-floor flat in a lovely area of Wimbledon. I did take the precaution of getting the advice of a builder because the flat was very damp and in a totally dilapidated state. To buy it I needed to raise the entire cost in the form of a mortgage secured against the flat I was living in. At the auction, I was practically the only female in the room and certainly the only woman actually bidding. It was incredibly exciting. And fast. When the gavel came down in my favour, my adrenaline levels had gone through the roof and I was totally exhilarated. I took a significant financial risk and I might have ended up homeless (two properties and an enormous mortgage to pay) but that catastrophe didn't happen. I loved the Wimbledon flat so much when the builder had renovated it that I sold the other flat and moved, mortgage-free, into a very much nicer home than I could otherwise have afforded.

/ We underestimate our ability to cope. If you are full of self-doubt and lack confidence, it's very easy to think, 'Oh no, I couldn't cope if I took a chance and such and such a thing happened.' It is not uncommon for women to underestimate their capabilities and yet, time and again when tested, most of the women I know have shown quite remarkable strength. I watched my daughter become a tigress when her baby daughter was sick for months in hospital. In the past five years she has taken so many risks to confront the medical and social care system to advocate on India's behalf. The result is that India's development has surpassed all expectations and Suzy has ensured that India is now at a special school perfect for her complex needs.

1/ If I do nothing, what will it be like a year from now?

2/ Why is my fear causing me to overestimate the risk and underestimate myself, and holding me back?

What Will You Risk?

There is no growth without risk. Maybe you are already feeling slightly overwhelmed by the notion of taking any risk at all – so let's just consider what level of risk you might be prepared to take. Some risks are less momentous than others. Some risks are quick and easy to take. Some are major life decisions and some may be beyond the realms of possibility for you at the moment because of your personal circumstances. As with every suggestion in this book, these are intended to help you to get clarity, to spark ideas and to stimulate your imagination.

One

/

THE RISK OF MOVING LOCATION

So much easier to stay put in familiar surroundings, literally plodding along the paths well travelled for many years. Or is it preferable to explore pastures new and find opportunities to see the world from a different perspective? A less risky option if you live in an interesting place might be to do a house swap with people in other parts of the world. This might also give you the opportunity to try somewhere new before committing to it full-time.

Two

/

THE RISK OF A NEW RELATIONSHIP

I have just heard a news item about the increasing numbers of the over-sixty-fives who are getting married, and I am full of admiration for people taking that risk either for the second or maybe first time in their lives. The complications of forming a new relationship, especially after leaving another relationship or losing a loved one, must be very daunting. There are likely to be many practical considerations as well as offspring on both sides who might have something to say about the new relationship and may put up objections. A close friend of mine has just married a widower she met at a language class. She had also lost her lifetime partner and after a few years was open to a new love. They are both entirely happy and all their friends and family are delighted for them. I acknowledge and celebrate their bravery.

Three

/

THE RISK OF STARTING A NEW VENTURE

If you have been in business or you have some talent or skill you feel you could either sell or share with others for money, then you might consider creating a new business around it. Because this is the particular risk I have had most experience of during my third act, these are the key considerations before you start:

◆ Do your research before you start but also trust your gut.

◆ How big is the market? Will it be local, regional or international?

◆ How will you tell people about your goods or services?

◆ How much can you afford to risk and potentially lose?

◆ What will you need to do before you can start to make money?

◆ What skills or knowledge do you lack and who can supply those?

◆ What will you do if it grows fast? Are you ambitious for success?

◆ How will you feel if it doesn't succeed?

I'd like to tell you that I did very careful planning and preparation before I took the first steps to launch LFF, but in many ways I just trusted my gut instinct that there'd be many women who felt like me about the beauty industry.

I did think, 'What's the worst that could happen?' Obviously I had to work out my finances very carefully. I decided I would limit my investment to an amount I could afford to lose, because I would not have time to make that money back via any employed income. After my initial investment, I relied on OPMs (other people's money) by offering them a stake in Look Fabulous Forever. This means that I no longer own 100 per cent of the business, but that's a small price to pay for being able to sleep at night!

Four

/

THE RISK OF LEARNING SOMETHING NEW

This might include a form of physical activity like yoga, Pilates, Tai Chi or dancing. Maybe you want to learn a language or take up an instrument or join a choir. Perhaps you could take on a period of study for a qualification, from A-level to a degree or a higher degree. How about study and travel combined so that you take a course in, say, architecture that then takes you to interesting architectural sites? It could be as simple as enrolling for the U3A (University of the Third Age) to see what is available in your area. This may feel like a lesser risk but it also requires belief, commitment and effort. However, the rewards are potentially very great, and following a course of study opens the possibility of meeting lots of new people of all ages, and also of feeling pride in whatever qualification (or satisfaction) you achieve.

Five

/

THE RISK OF A NEW HOBBY

Is there something you have always wanted to do? Write a book or throw a clay pot or paint a glorious sunset? This is all about unscratched itches and starts with the words: 'I wish I could . . .' or 'I'd love to be able to . . .' I applaud television programmes like *The Great British Bake Off*, *The Great Pottery Throw Down* and *The Great British Sewing Bee* because they always include older people having a go. And doing so on television in front of millions! How I admire them and how often they are brilliantly talented and sometimes even win the show. When I have time in a few years I intend to resume my hobby of photography and do some more courses, preferably overseas.

Six

/

THE RISK OF INTREPID TRAVEL

Travelling is high on most older people's lists of things to do and may stretch no further than going on a wonderful cruise. For others, this is the opportunity to see the Great Wall of China or Machu Picchu or any number of places they have always wanted to visit. Or how about a gap year with only a backpack? The possibilities are endless and there'll never be a better time. I had a very life-affirming email from a customer recently. Her son had asked her to research a demanding hiking trip through Switzerland. He is super-fit so she came up with a great itinerary to suit his needs. Then he suggested that she and her husband might like to accompany him. So, with some trepidation and a few what-ifs, they went as well and loved every minute.

Seven

/

THE RISK OF CHANGING YOUR APPEARANCE

This could be something apparently trivial (to others but probably not to you) like allowing your hair to go grey, or something major like embarking on a long-term weight-loss programme or starting an exercise regime when you have never done anything remotely sporty before. Again, I have some experience of the latter, having decided to get fit for the first time in my life at sixty-nine. I haven't found it easy and many times in the past months I have come close to failure, but I will keep going. I want to have more control over how well I age so there is no alternative – giving up isn't an option.

This is in no way an exhaustive list, but I hope I have given you some ideas that 'spark your joy'. Since I took the risk to start Look Fabulous Forever, I have had the best fun of my life. My age has been the biggest advantage, partly because of all the experience I have been able to bring from a long life doing lots of different things. I have met very many different people of all ages, and have had to learn many new techie things, surprising myself almost every day with my capacity to do so. It has shown me that our brains are capable of a great degree of plasticity. I may have far fewer brain cells than I did forty years ago but I can still learn when I need to. It wasn't the objective, but I feel five years younger than I did five years ago instead of five years older. My life is full of purpose and now I know how I am going to 'get through' the next thirty years. I am going to live and savour every last second of the bonus of time that I have left to me. I am going to live the life more fabulous! Why not join me?

SUE'S STORY

'GOSH, YOU'RE BRAVE,' said a friend when I told her we were moving. 'Brave or stupid?' I laughed. But there was just never any doubt. Once we'd agreed that we didn't want to end our lives without living in Cornwall, it was something that just had to happen. We understood there'd be risks – moving away from the area you've lived in for over forty years, from your friendly GP, let alone friends; a risk to move to a new county where, yes, you'd visited time and time and time again over the years, where you knew one or two people but had no one close; a risk, at the end of your sixties, to move 250 miles away from your family. But within six months of taking the decision in principle we were here, arriving at the end of a dreary February to our new home.

We moved to a hamlet a mile back from the coast we loved. We were within six miles, or ten minutes, of a small town, within five minutes of wonderful beaches. Although we hadn't intended doing much at all to our new home, we found ourselves busy in the first year changing a staircase, taking out a wall, ripping out the kitchen. The garden, surrounded by fields, had been rather neglected and so our arms became scratched as we battled with brambles and ivy.

At least twice a day we walked the dogs, often putting them in the car and zooming to a beach where we could all enjoy the dunes and rock pools and chasing balls. But we also did the shorter walks around the village, up the old track to the church, turning round to look out on the ocean, watching the birds, bats, bees, enjoying the wildflowers – and the peace and huge skies. As we walked we met other dog walkers and wherever we went we said hello to people. Gradually, we would stop and talk; we joined a group cleaning the beach; we joined another group and found ourselves helping with village events.

Friends and family came and stayed – at times it felt as if we were running a B&B, with one lot leaving as another arrived! It was lovely to see everyone and share our new surroundings. Time with family was no longer just a lunch or cup of tea, and we've found ourselves spending more time talking. The grandchildren (ten under ten) are hopefully going to grow up with the same love we have for this area, coming down to us during school holidays.

We've been here a year now and we're really enjoying the different pace of life, lack of traffic, different priorities. We go back 'up country' every few weeks to see the families, but our roots are growing down here now. If we hadn't taken the risk then, there would always have been the 'if only' or 'I wish'. We're both seventy this summer and are looking forward to a good few years living somewhere we both really want to be.

Conclusion

When I set out to write this handbook I was already excited about the prospect of really making the most of my third act of life. Having spoken to lots of different people and read widely on the implications of living for upwards of ninety years, I have come to several conclusions:

1 /

The third act used to be relatively short and was called 'retirement' because it was seen as the beginning of the end of life. It is now relatively long and can be seen as the beginning of a whole new phase of life.

2 /

We are fortunate to belong to the first generation to be (almost) guaranteed to have this extended period during which we can really explore how to make the most of it.

3 /

Our grandparents and parents are not useful role models for how to live the life more fabulous as we age. We are in uncharted territory, so we need new maps and new signposts. I also think that we need new attitudes and beliefs about our ageing selves.

4 /

Our society has not yet come to terms with increased longevity. Politicians and the media invariably talk about 'the ageing population' in the most negative terms as 'problems', 'burdens' and 'costs' – especially in health and social care.

5 /

We can massively influence how well we age in the choices we make and the decisions we take. By changing our attitudes, behaviours and lifestyle we can greatly improve the quality of our lives.

The real challenge is how to ensure that our much longer lives are as healthy as possible. When I say this, I am sure that most of you will be thinking in terms of 'not getting ill', but this is a very narrow definition and I prefer the one proposed by the World Health Organization in 1948: 'Health is a state of complete physical, mental and social wellbeing and not merely the absence of disease or infirmity.' This definition encompasses the idea that caring for your appearance, feeling confident about yourself and having good social relationships are emblematic of true health. I would also suggest that we need to find a way to accommodate the notion of growing older and that currently we can take one of three approaches:

BY DENYING OR EFFACING IT

This is superficially very attractive, especially to people in their second act or midlife. In this approach there is no acceptance of ageing. The core belief is that with sufficient effort ageing can be postponed indefinitely, so there is no acknowledgement or recognition of the physical, mental or emotional changes that come with age. Everything possible is done to create a youthful appearance. Faces and bodies are sculpted with surgery and exercise regimes in an attempt to remove any signs of ageing and one's chronological age is a dirty little secret which you share with no one, although in this day and age everyone will know perfectly well how old you are!

The watchwords of this approach are 'ANTI-AGEING' and 'AGELESS STYLE', and the key mantra is: 'NO ONE KNOWS MY REAL AGE'.

BY THROWING IN
THE TOWEL

This is also attractive to many as they age because it requires little effort and involves a surrender to the inevitable process of withdrawal and invisibility that comes with living in an ageist society. It is the polar opposite of the first approach. The core belief is that ageing confers the right to be excused from meaningful engagement with the modern world or from any responsibility for one's own health and wellbeing.

The watchwords of this approach are defeatist: 'NOBODY CARES WHAT I LOOK LIKE' and 'WHAT'S THE POINT?'; and the key mantra is: 'I'M TOO OLD TO CHANGE'.

BY LIVING THE LIFE
MORE FABULOUS

This is the ultimate expression of positive ageing and it's about staying fully engaged with everything around us but on our own terms. I accept that this approach will hold little attraction for the age-deniers or the age-capitulators; however, I truly hope it appeals to all of you who might be feeling confused and slightly lost in this new landscape. You will be the ones who haven't thrown in the towel, but neither have you any desire to be mistaken for your own daughter! The core belief of the fabulous approach is that we accept and value our ageing selves, just as we rather like buildings and objects that show some signs of age. In this philosophy, we take full responsibility for our own wellbeing in our lifestyle choices and are still open to learning, growth and whatever

opportunities come our way, because we love life and want to
live it to the full.

**Watchwords are 'JOIE DE VIVRE' and 'PERSONAL STYLE',
and the key mantra is: 'AGE IS NO BARRIER TO FABULOUSNESS'.**

I hope you agree that this third approach is a good compromise
between trying too hard and not trying hard enough to age positively.
I also hope you have enjoyed reading this book as much as I have
enjoyed writing it. My intention was to give you as many practical
ideas as I could to help you to have the very best 'third age' that you
can possibly achieve. I wanted it to transform your attitudes to your
makeup, hair and style in order to help you to look more fabulous.
I wanted it to inspire you to take more exercise and make better
nutritional choices in order to help you to feel more fabulous, and I
wanted it to empower you to become more confident and open to
new opportunities in order to help you to live a more adventurous
life. I started optimistic and excited about the possibility of 'living the
life more fabulous' and became even more so in the course of the
research I have done into various aspects of growing older. I have
come to realise that ageing is not a terrifying monster that we need to
fight or to which we need to passively submit. It is a gradual process of
adaptation to changes that we can meet with resilience, energy and
– even – a spirit of enquiry and adventure. So here's to a long, happy
and above all fabulous life!

Acknowledgements

My first acknowledgment needs to go to all the very many older women who have engaged with me since I started Look Fabulous Forever. You are a fabulous and powerful 'tribe' and I so appreciate your encouragement and support.

My thanks to Luigi Bonomi and Danielle Zigner at LBA without whose wise direction this book would never have come to fruition. I have also very much enjoyed working with my editor, Olivia Morris and the team at Orion who have been delightfully open to all my suggestions and who have (practically) indulged my every whim. It was a pleasure to work closely with Nikki Dupin and Simon Songhurst on the design and photography and to see my suggestions and ideas translated by them into beautiful reality on the page.

I was also helped by a number of people who gave me the benefit of their time, knowledge and expertise, so my heartfelt thanks go to Elizabeth Bessant, Michaela Mitoi, Jody Bradford, Nathan Walker, Trevor Sorbie, Lindsay Burrows, Leonie Wright, Barbara Crisp, Josephine Wilkinson, Rosemary Hurtley and Dr. Edward Kelly.

I would not have been able to write this book without my team at LFF who allowed me the time and space to devote to it, so a huge thank you to Anna, Caroline, Sam, Diana, Suzy, Alida, Verity, Julie and Debbie for holding the fort so magnificently.

And finally I'd like to acknowledge my truly exceptional friends and family who have never once suggested that I am completely bonkers to be starting a new business at sixty-five and writing my first book at sixty-nine!